SUCCEEDING AT BUSINESS AND TECHNICAL PRESENTATIONS

SUCCEEDING AT BUSINESS AND TECHNICAL PRESENTATIONS

Second Edition

Leonard F. Meuse, Jr.

JOHN WILEY & SONS

New York • Chichester • Brisbane • Toronto • Singapore

HF
5718
M485
1988

This publication is designed to provide accurate and
authoritative information in regard to the subject
matter covered. It is sold with the understanding that
the publisher is not engaged in rendering legal, accounting,
or other professional service. If legal advice or other
expert assistance is required, the services of a competent
professional person should be sought. *From a Declaration
of Principles jointly adopted by a Committee of the
American Bar Association and a Committee of Publishers.*

Library of Congress Cataloging in Publication Data:

Meuse, Leonard F., 1933–
    Succeeding at business and technical presentations / by Leonard F.
Meuse, Jr.   2nd. Ed.
    p.   cm.
    Bibliography: p.
    ISBN 0-471-62486-1
    1. Business communication.   2. Oral communication.   3. Public
speaking.   I. Title.
HF5718.M485   1989   88-14866
805.5'1—dc19   CIP

Printed in the United States of America

10 9 8 7 6 5 4 3 2 1

To My Wife and Family

PREFACE

This book expands my 1980 work, *Mastering the Business and Technical Presentation*. The initial impulse for tackling the project came from an awareness that personal computers, which were uncommon in business, government, and the universities in 1980, had not only become everyday tools, they were also changing the ways we create business and technical graphics, produce visuals for presentations, and even project images for audiences. Clearly, an update was needed to explain the new tools and the new choices now available.

But beyond this first impulse, the experience and insights of the past eight years compelled a fresh view of the entire process of planning, preparing, and delivering business and technical presentations.

Thus, a new chapter deals with producing visual aids—not just with a personal computer, but covering the entire range from producing visuals on a shoestring budget to tips on using professional audiovisual services. The chapter on designing visuals has detailed guides for selecting and creating effective business and technical graphics, the use of color, readability, and professional appearance.

The book has new tips on becoming an effective communicator in general and communicating successfully with audiences in particular. It contains a section to help speakers sound more forceful and persuasive by avoiding vague, tentative language. It provides checklists of commonly mispronounced and poorly enunciated words and phrases. The book deals not only with how to construct logical and persuasive arguments, but how convincingly to refute arguments as well. The information on managing nervous energy and coping with stage fright has doubled and now contains practical tips on how to prepare mentally and physically. The chapter on delivery has been expanded to include many new tips on reaching and holding audiences—for example, how to use audiovisual and presentation equipment (pointers, projectors, lecterns, easel pads, microphones). Techniques on introducing a speaker and how to organize and conduct team presentations have also been added.

In short, the present work reflects a more *current* view of the changing world of audiovisual design, creation, and practice along with a more *complete* view of something that changes very little but yields new secrets with each passing year: the science and the art of human communication.

LEONARD F. MEUSE, JR.

Chelmsford, Massachusetts
June 1988

ACKNOWLEDGMENTS

My thanks go to my wife, Dot, whose patience and support made this book possible. My gratitude goes also to the hundreds of speakers and audiences with whom I have worked. These pages are filled with the things we taught each other.

L.F.M.

INTRODUCTION

HOW TO CREATE A DISASTER

Perhaps you feel that turning your presentation into the second maiden voyage of the *Titanic* is easy. You're wrong; it takes dedication, imagination, inspiration, and, most of all, unswerving courage. Let me describe just a few of the methods:

- Don't waste time by considering the *objective* of your presentation. Get down to business immediately.
- Don't engage in futile exercises such as *analyzing your audience's background, attitudes, and needs*. These intellectual games serve only to confuse and immobilize you.
- Don't consider *strategy*. When you deliver the presentation, your persuasive powers will win the day.
- Never lose precious time in *organizing* your information. No one bothers with such things as outlines these days. Even if you do make an outline, you probably won't use it anyway. Plan something today and the situation will change tomorrow, rendering the plan useless.
- Whatever you do, don't prepare a *script*. There's no time for that. Besides, it's overkill. The important thing is to get some visuals that you can talk to. Some of the visuals are probably available from old presentations you have done.
- If you start worrying about such trivial things as *physical factors*— rooms, projectors, screens, seating, lighting, acoustics—you will take valuable time away from your important duties. Remember, your job comes first!
- Don't be overly concerned about *delivering* the presentation. This too is a waste of time. Just get up and speak your piece. You don't have to be an actor to explain accounts receivable, computer simulations, or lab experiments.

- Don't use fancy visuals. They will make you look like you're in show business. Use existing documents and working papers as much as possible. Avoid the use of graphics. They oversimplify things.
- Never have a dry run. This wastes not just your time, but also that of everyone else involved. Moreover, your practice presentation may well turn out better than the real thing!
- Above all, don't get ready too soon. The longer you wait, the more current your data will be. By waiting until the last minute, you will invoke the pressures of a tight deadline—pressures that will help you achieve your best results.

If, on the other hand, you number yourself among the people who are not especially fond of disasters, the material in these pages will help you. This book is a field manual on achieving business, technical, and professional goals through communicating with audiences. It is a compilation of tactics, suggestions, ideas, tips, checklists, and biases accumulated over many years of working with speakers and audiences. The goal is not to be theoretical— full of high sounding, profound insights—but to be practical and genuinely useful.

We will deal with two questions:

1. What is the best way to *prepare* a business, technical, or sales presentation?
2. What are the techniques for *delivering* presentations that will ensure success in informing and persuading audiences?

Much of the information in these pages is the product of memorable mistakes as well as gratifying successes. My aim is that you avoid the mistakes and create many successes of your own.

Please dog-ear the pages.

CONTENTS

ILLUSTRATIONS, *xix*

Chapter 1 WHAT'S IN IT FOR ME?, 1

Chapter 2 THE DYNAMICS OF A PRESENTATION, 3
Why a Presentation?, 4
The Range of Business and Technical Presentations, 5
A Special Power, 6
The Death of Writing?, 10
  Problem One: Presentations Disappear, 10
  Problem Two: Presentations Are Expensive and Work Best with
    Limited Audiences, 11
  Problem Three: The Pace Is Sender-Controlled, 11
How Formal Should Your Presentation Be?, 12
  Reasons for a More Formal Presentation, 13
  Requirements for a More Formal Presentation, 13

Chapter 3 DEFINE YOUR OBJECTIVE, 16
Why All This Talk of Behavior?, 17
Objectives Must Be Realistic, 20

Chapter 4 ANALYZE YOUR AUDIENCE, 22
Audience Background, 23
Audience Attitudes, 25
Obtaining the Information, 26
Communicating with an Audience, 27
Communication Is Sharing, 28
The Making of a Communicator, 29
  Desire, 29
  Work, 30
  Humility, 30

Chapter 5 CONSIDER YOUR TACTICS, *31*
How Many Presentations?, 31
Timing, 32
Who Should Attend?, 32
Preliminary Encounters, 33
Overcoming Obstacles to Achieving Your Goal, 34
   Adversaries, 34
   Negative Information, 35
The Tactical Frame of Mind, 35

Chapter 6 ORGANIZE YOUR INFORMATION, *36*
Why Bother?, 36
The Zoomie Packaging Company, 37
What Is the Problem?, 38
Organizing the Beginning, 40
   Who Are You?, 40
   What Are You Up To?, 40
   What Is the Scope of the Presentation?, 40
   What Are the Criteria?, 41
   What Do You Expect of Me?, 41
   What's in It for Me?, 41
The Middle, 42
G&T Company, Fairlawn Park, 43
   Organizing the G&T Presentation, 45
Exposition or Persuasion?, 48
Expository Patterns, 48
   Chronology, 49
   Analysis, 49
   Classification, 49
   Cause and Effect, 49
   Question and Answer, 49
Persuasive Patterns: Logic, 51
   Deduction, 51
   Induction, 52
   Analogy, 53
   Elimination, 53
Rebuttal, 54
Some Concluding Thoughts About Persuasion: Emotions, 55
   Fear, 55

Gain, 55
The Herd Instinct, 56
Testimonial, 56
Other Emotional Factors, 56
The Ending, 57
Outlining Techniques, 57

**Chapter 7   CREATE THE AUDIO AND THE VISUAL
               CHANNELS, 60**
Begin with a Script?, 60
Creating the Audio Channel, 63
A Good Script Communicates, 63
The Importance of Style, 64
How to Sound Uncertain, Tentative, Vague, and Imprecise, 65
Humor, 69
The Importance of Pace, 70
The Importance of Unity, 70
The Importance of Emphasis, 71
Helpful Hints on Writing the Audio Channel of Your Script, 72
Creating the Visual Channel, 73
What's a Visual?, 73
Visual Media: Which One Is Best for Me?, 73
Projected Media, 75
Nonprojected Media, 81
Which Visual Medium?, 84
Choosing Effective Visuals, 84
General Rules for Effective Visuals, 84
The Importance of Balance, 87
Overloading, 88
Weak Visual Channel, 88
Failure to Integrate the Two Channels, 88
The Most Overlooked Reason for Preparing a Script, 89
Choices, 90

Chapter 8   PRODUCE YOUR VISUALS, 91
Visuals on a Shoestring, 91
Computer-Generated Presentation Graphics, 93
Using Professional Audiovisual Services, 99
Using Audiovisual Services Effectively, 99

Types Of Visuals,   100
  Text Slides,   100
  Tables,   102
  Statistical Graphics,   103
  Diagrams and Schematics,   111
  Using Color,   113
Visuals for Technical Presentations,   116
Getting Help,   117

Chapter 9   CONSIDER THE PHYSICAL FACTORS,   118
The Room,   118
Arranging the Seats and Audiovisual Equipment,   120
What Time?,   125
How Long?,   126
The Other Equipment,   127
Other Necessities,   128
Remember Murphy,   128

Chapter 10   DELIVER YOUR PRESENTATION,   129
What Is So Difficult?,   129
The Quest for Perfection,   130
Trying to Be Someone Else,   131
Overall Rules for Effective Delivery,   132
  Rule One: Engagement,   132
  Rule Two: Energy,   132
  Rule Three: Empathy,   133
  Impact on Delivery,   133
  Rule Four: Keep Going,   134
  Rule Five: Manage Your Nervous Energy,   136
  Five Guideposts to Effective Delivery,   143
Effective Delivery Techniques,   144
  Style,   145
  The Voice,   145
  The Body,   155
Appearance,   162
How to Use Visuals and Audiovisual Equipment,   163
  Using Visuals,   163
  Using a Lectern,   167
  Using a Microphone,   168

Tone,   168
Handling Questions,   169
 When Do You Want Questions?,   169
 Q&A Should Be a Group Process,   171
 Take Your Time,   172
 Do's and Don'ts for Handling Questions,   172
 Special Challenges,   174
Putting It All Together,   177

Chapter 11   OTHER THOUGHTS,   178
A Dry Run,   178
Four Methods of Addressing an Audience,   179
Giving an Impromptu Speech,   180
Reading a Speech,   180
Team Presentations,   182
Delivering an Introduction,   184
Presentations by Handicapped Persons,   184
Using Videotape,   185
The Value of Preparation,   185
Luck,   185

INDEX,   187

ILLUSTRATIONS

TABLES

Table 1   Advantages and Disadvantages of Audiovisual
             Communication,   12
Table 2   Comparing Degrees of Formality,   14
Table 3   Selecting a Visual Medium,   85
Table 4   First Draft Prepared with a Typewriter,   104
Table 5   Final Typeset Draft,   105

FIGURES

Figure 1   The Communication Process,   28
Figure 2   Three Classes of Information,   39
Figure 3   Main Theme and Supporting Themes,   58
Figure 4   Final Outline,   58
Figure 5   A Sample Script,   62
Figure 6   Explaining the Pythagorean Theorem,   74
Figure 7   Two Types of Overhead Projector,   77
Figure 8   LCD Projection System,   81
Figure 9   Typewriter vs. Laser Printer,   94
Figure 10   Chart, Paint, and Draw Computer Graphics,   96, 97
Figure 11   Pointing and Drawing Devices,   98
Figure 12   Key Words Only,   101
Figure 13   Using Bar Graphs,   106
Figure 14   Bar Chart Basics,   108
Figure 15   Line Graphs,   109
Figure 16   Pie Chart Techniques,   111
Figure 17   Diagrams and Schematics,   112
Figure 18   Speaker Near the Doorway,   121
Figure 19   Speaker Opposite the Doorway,   122
Figure 20   Typical Room Arrangements,   123
Figure 21   Optimum Times for Presentations,   126
Figure 22   Four Positions to Avoid,   159

SUCCEEDING AT BUSINESS AND TECHNICAL PRESENTATIONS

1

What's In It for Me?

It's a fair question. After all, reading anything is a considerable investment in these days of instant electronic communications. It's reasonable to mention the returns you can expect from *your* investment.

Most professionals receive no training in presentation skills. Yet, with few exceptions, such skills are essential to success in every professional field. True, professions are largely about ideas. But an important part of being a professional involves explaining your ideas and convincing others of their validity and worth. And much of that explaining and convincing is done with groups of peers, clients, prospects, and superiors in formal and informal presentations.

Whether by design or by happenstance, presentation skills are one of the measures by which professionals and managers are evaluated.

The ability to prepare and conduct presentations is also an essential management skill, even though most business schools don't include presentation training in the core curriculum. Many men and women begin their careers as professionals and, because of their abilities and aptitudes, find themselves in management. Suddenly, the need to communicate with groups of people becomes an important part of the workday—despite the lack of formal training.

1

Perhaps you have been giving presentations for many years and wish to be more effective. Perhaps you are an experienced speaker who makes frequent presentations to the board of directors or the top-level executive committee in your organization on high-stakes issues and programs. You may have been asking yourself questions similar to these:

- What elements of my preparation and delivery can be improved?
- How can I deal with nervousness?
- What constitutes an effective visual aid?
- What are the techniques for using audiovisual aids?
- Should I use humor?
- What is the best way to deal with questions?
- How do I conduct group discussions?
- How do I handle interruptions?
- What facets of effective presentations have I never considered?
- What are the pitfalls I should avoid?

Presentation skills fall broadly into two categories: preparation and delivery.

In preparing a presentation you need to know all the questions to ask. You need to complete as many of the steps as you have time for—things that you must do *before the presentation actually begins* to assure success. You must also plan what you expect will happen *after the presentation is over* as next steps on the path toward achieving your goals.

Delivery involves all of the things you do with your voice and your body to establish a rapport with your audience and to communicate with it. Communicating with an audience requires sending clear messages and *receiving* them as well. Delivery involves not just speaking to an audience, but also conducting group discussions and handling questions.

If you are a member of any of the groups described above and have asked yourself questions similar to those listed—welcome. "What's in it for you" is the ability to ask and answer all the questions needed to prepare a successful presentation and a guide on how to communicate with audiences.

I hope to make the information equally useful for members of large organizations with many available resources as well as for individual consultants or entrepreneurs who must operate with limited means.

One's budget need affect neither quality, nor the most important ingredient of all—intellectual substance.

2

The Dynamics of a Presentation

L et's begin with a few definitions of the terms that apply to presentations. An *audiovisual presentation* is a communications medium in which the audience receives messages through two channels: the eyes and the ears. This book is a practical guide on how to reach audiences through *live* audiovisual presentations. For brevity, this book will use the single word *presentation* instead of audiovisual presentation. Besides being a communication through two channels, a presentation is a deliberate act in which carefully planned and programmed sounds and images focus the attention of an audience on a subject for a brief period. It is this designed collaboration of auditory and visual impressions that can give a presentation the power to hold an audience's attention and, more important, to inform and persuade them.

A *speech* is a presentation without a planned visual channel. The audience receives visual information, of course, but at random. The principal focus is the speaker. An effective speaker can provide enough visual interest to hold the attention of an audience, but the lack of a *programmed* visual channel allows the audience to spend much of its time concentrating on trivialities, such as the color of the speaker's tie, the shape of the lighting fixture, or the expressions on the faces of other people.

3

A *meeting* usually has less structure (and, sadly, less direction) than either a presentation or a speech. At meetings, the *presenter* and the *audience* are in constant flux, because each attendee is expected to both listen and contribute. It is important to mention meetings here for two reasons. First, the presentation is often used as a prelude to a meeting. The meeting burgeons naturally out of the presentation as a review and discussion of its content and an agreement on what action must be taken. We will deal later with the challenge of preventing a presentation from becoming a meeting prematurely. Second, in many meetings, *visuals* are used to focus attention on a problem or question or on project data. The audience works on the problem or reviews the data using the projected image as a visual worksheet. The use of a projector does not turn these meetings into presentations.

To repeat: A presentation consists of a series of *deliberately planned* sounds and images and, for our purposes, is delivered live to an audience.

WHY A PRESENTATION?

Do you really need to give a presentation? Other less expensive methods of conveying your message are at your disposal. Why not write a memo? Or report? Why not make a series of phone calls, or simply have a meeting?

To begin with, it's important to recognize the hierarchical value of the various communications methods used in organizations. At the bottom of the heap is the memo or written report sent in the company mail. The underlying (and perhaps unintended) message is that the subject can't be urgent or overwhelmingly important. If it were, the sender would not have taken the time to compose and type it and then leave its fate to the vagaries of the company mail! The same can be said of electronic mail, which is really a medium for sending short messages. Here, the delivery system may be quicker and surer than paper mail, but the *receiver* has to initiate the completion of the communication.

Phone calls are a notch up in the hierarchy. Because of the need to discuss a subject directly, they confer a sense of immediacy and importance (at least on the part of the caller). Next higher in the communications rankings is the appointment. Here one takes the time and trouble to schedule a meeting to engage in face-to-face communication. (The informal, "drop by" meeting ranks lower. The person being dropped in on is likely to be busy or not even present.) Moving upward, we come to meetings. They have the same dynamics as appointments but with the added need for *several* people to interact in person. Finally, the most prestigious medium of organizational communication is the presentation. It carries all the status of the meeting, but adds to it the time and effort spent in organizing and creating the audiovisual program itself.

Think of the hierarchy of communications media when you are choosing a method to convey your message. The method you choose is part of the message. Written communication is not limited to lesser tasks, such as monthly reports and requests for paper clips; it is just better suited for communications that don't require timely, personal interaction. Phone calls have their place, too; but when the stakes are high enough, face-to-face communication is indispensable. Meetings are useful for obtaining group understanding or approval and even for working on a problem. But they lack the focus, direction, and impact that a presentation can provide.

We are slow to acknowledge the power of the presentation. A presentation is often called a "Dog and Pony Show" or a "Show and Tell" in organizational circles. (After all, we are in business—not "Show Business.") Yet the predominant form of structured communication in large business and government organizations is the presentation. In fact, if you are a vice president or above in a major corporation, it is likely that much of your workday is spent attending presentations and participating in the decisions that emerge from them.

THE RANGE OF BUSINESS AND TECHNICAL PRESENTATIONS

For convenience, we can classify business and technical presentations as falling into one or more of the following categories (with examples):

1. Review
   Unit performance
   Progress report
   Achievements against goals
   Program or project review
2. Proposal
   New (or modification to) program, product, policy, procedure, system (information, administrative, technical)
   Organizational or operational change
   Strategic
3. Information Sharing
   Explain organization (mission, membership, activities, plans)
   Explain system (administrative, technical)
   Orientation (organization, product)
   Training (technical, nontechnical)
   Explain policies, procedures, practices, benefits, expectations

> Brainstorming
> Problem solving
> 4. Motivational
>> Sales meetings
>> Product introductions
>> Product sales presentations
>> Launching a new project or program
>> Thank you
>> Congratulations, awards for achievement

The categories are not meant to be watertight. For example, a new product proposal can contain elements of information sharing. They do, however, represent a way of capturing the vast range of business and technical presentations in a systematic way.

And in this system, how does one differentiate between business and technical presentations? Technical presentations can fall into any of the four categories. The first three are straightforward. One can easily imagine *technical* reviews, proposals, and information sharing. True, most motivational presentations are not technical, but even here, it is not rare to see a motivational presentation dealing with detailed technical product or project information.

In the last analysis, what makes a presentation "technical" is technical subject matter. The presenter of a technical presentation has a background in the technologies being discussed. The audience may *or may not*. The distinctions between the two pure types are easily blurred. New product presentations, for example, usually begin with a technical feasibility analysis and go on to include a business plan. In such cases, the content of the presentation is both technical and business related. The important point to bear in mind is this: *The rules and techniques for creating and delivering effective presentations apply equally to both categories, business and technical.*

A SPECIAL POWER

Why are presentations so pervasive in industry, commerce, and government? One reason is *feedback*. What little feedback you get from memos and reports is often days or even weeks in coming. Presentations give you immediate information—and not just on your proposal, plan, idea, or request. Other kinds of useful messages, both spoken and unspoken, are available as people react and interact.

"I disagree."
"I don't understand."
"I'm bored."

"It's a good plan if you can convince my boss."
"I like your idea."

You need two levels of feedback in any communications situation. The first level concerns how well your audience has received and understood your message. The second deals with how that audience reacts to the information. The presentation has the powerful advantage of gathering all the participants involved in a proposed course of action or all the principals in a decision-making process and achieving one or more of the following results:

1. Ensuring uniform understanding
2. Reaching group judgment
3. Obtaining the reaction of a group (e.g., to a problem)
4. Solving a problem (or pointing one out)
5. Obtaining approval (e.g., budget, proposal, program)
6. Arriving at a decision
7. Gaining acceptance for a project, idea, plan, or scheme
8. Resolving conflicts
9. Assigning responsibility
10. Energizing and motivating people

What makes a presentation special is that *people* convene to focus their energies on a subject and usually to interact. The presenter gets immediate feedback, and so do the participants.

Another reason for the widespread use of presentations in large organizations is *impact*. You could write a report, for example, and in the conclusion section state, "Resolution of the corrosion problem is of paramount importance to the reduction of customer returns with its current negative impact on margins as well as its potential long-range threat to sales." In an oral presentation you do not have time to create long, complex sentences with big words. Oral communication tends to be more direct and visceral. In a presentation you would likely summarize your findings more powerfully: "This corrosion problem is serious, and we'd better solve it quickly. Customer returns are already slashing into our margins. If we don't fix the problem soon, sales will begin to suffer, too."

As contrasted with writing, the immediacy of a presentation allows you to be more spontaneous, more yourself. The audience in part responds to *you* as opposed to your words on paper. The voice adds depth and dimension to the words. The changes in pitch, loudness, inflection, animation, vocal pace; the use of pauses; the vocal emphasis—all these factors contribute to the overall message received, conveying information beyond the mere words.

The traffic this morning was *unbelievable*.

Occasionally, as in the previous sentence, the words alone are ambiguous until uttered by a human voice. Only by listening can we tell if the traffic was unbelievably good or bad.

Beyond speech dynamics, a large part of the impact of a presentation is visual. In an audiovisual presentation the audience is absorbing and processing what it sees as well as what it hears. Part of the impact is in the visuals themselves—the charts, graphs, diagrams, and illustrations, which will be discussed in detail later. But *you* are part of the visual channel as well. Your appearance, posture, facial expressions, gestures—in fact, anything you do with your body—becomes visual information and is part of the total impact of the presentation.

The third reason for the popularity of presentations is *control*.

When you write a memo or report, you surrender it to the reader. What will be its fate? Will it be read carefully? Will it be read at all? What distractions in the reader's environment or preoccupations in the reader's mind will interfere with the communication of your message? In an audiovisual presentation, you have the advantage of a captive audience. You have prepared the physical setting to enhance communication. True, some people may leave the room mentally, but if you work at preparation and if your delivery skills are working, you can exert a great deal of control over how your message is received.

On a basic level, the audience is present in the room and has the choice of listening to you (a mental activity) or just hearing you (a physical activity). But beyond that, a presentation is a deliberate act. At its best, it is a carefully planned sequence of sounds and images. It is a programmed focusing on a subject for a brief period. Part of its power derives from the fact that the careful integration of audio and visual messages not only provides interest, it also produces a momentum that can compel the attention of an audience—in short, *control*.

The final advantage of the audiovisual presentation is that it is *easier* than reading. Most people prefer to get information from a presentation— even a canned presentation—rather than from reading. To "get information" is to learn. Learning is a three-part process:

1. *Recognition*—Receiving and identifying the physical signals that bear information.
2. *Association*—Relating the signals to our total experience. More simply, this step involves "pulling the file" we keep on each signal, reviewing the contents of that file, and relating it to the immediate situation.
3. *Understanding*—A new awareness based on the patterns formed by all the signals in a message.

Why the use of *signal* and not *word?* Because most of what we learn is based not just on words, but on *nonverbal* signals—gestures, facial expressions, body language, vocal intonations. Words on paper cannot possess the richness and variety of nonverbal communication. The reader is thus deprived of both the *information* and the *stimulation* that nonverbal signals provide.

At the basic level of recognition (step 1), it requires less *physical* work to listen to words than it does to read them. Anyone who has had the late evening experience of fighting to keep the eyelids open and struggling to drive the eyes across the rigid lines of text, page after page, knows that reading can be hard work.

Of course, physical factors can make listening a difficult task as well. A speaker's volume, pace, articulation, and vocal dynamics can affect listenability; so can the acoustics of the room. But except for extreme problem cases, listening is *physically* easier than the rigid, linear, one-dimensional demands of reading.

Can a person associate signals better when listening as opposed to reading?

Have you ever had the experience of "reading" a book and suddenly discovering that you don't have the vaguest notion of what you "read" in the last three paragraphs? Perhaps this is an unfair question. No doubt you have occasionally been "listening" to a speaker and experienced similar lapses. Association is hard work no matter how we receive the signals. Association is the mental work we must do to create meaning from the physical signals that comprise communication. Many factors can affect the process, including our energy level, our interest in the subject, the importance of the information to us, the degree of credibility we assign to the source, the presence or absence of distractions, bias, and preoccupation. These factors can frustrate communication for reader and listener alike.

But in an *effective* presentation, the immediacy, the dynamics, the interplay of verbal and nonverbal signals, the power of combining visual and vocal information can help audience members focus on the material. In short, the same factors that give a speaker a measure of control over the communication process also help the audience do its work of recognizing, associating, and understanding.

Why the pervasive reliance on the audiovisual presentation in organizations of every sort? Because it works. The presentation is a highly effective communications medium. It permits immediate feedback, helps the speaker to communicate with the impact of two-channel immediacy, allows a measure of control over the communication process and makes it easier for the audience to focus its attention and process the information.

THE DEATH OF WRITING?

Those who are keeping score are aware that writing has not put many points on the board. Is writing a dying craft to be practiced in the twenty-first century by pockets of monk-like specialists called neo-scribes? Will presentations become the ubiquitous communications form?

Presentations are *not* the answer to every business communication problem. Writing is not dying; it doesn't even have a cold! Presentations do have some serious disadvantages, three of which will be discussed here.

Problem One: Presentations Disappear

Since they consist of spoken words and brief images, presentations are impermanent phenomena. Your audience will recall perhaps 30 percent of the material in a presentation after one hour. Within a week, 95 percent will be forgotten. An audience typically remembers the main theme of a presentation along with four or five major supporting themes. They remember significant highlights, never the details.

Presentations are useless as reference sources.

High on the list of errors that even experienced presenters make is *overestimating the amount of detail an audience can remember*. Because we are familiar with our material, we assume that an audience can absorb and remember far more facts, numbers, and other supporting data than is remotely possible. Some presenters who are aware of this limitation provide the audience with "hard copy" (made on the office copier) of the visuals. But as you will see in detail later, if the visuals are well designed, they will not be useful as reference documents. They will contain only the *essence* of the ideas presented. You, the speaker, will provide most of the supporting detail. Conversely, visuals that contain all the detail to be covered by the speaker are usually disastrous as visuals. They become a written report that happens to be projected on the screen—one unreadable page after another. Haven't you attended more than one such presentation?

If achieving your communications goal requires providing reference material, *write it*. Writing provides a record. The business purpose of a communication often requires the permanency of a written document. A business plan, for example, is hardly likely to exist in oral form. Presentations, no matter how influential they may be in affecting the course of an organization, leave no record; they leave a series of impressions that begin eroding the moment the audience leaves the room. You may choose to overcome this limitation by providing your audience with a carefully prepared reference document that will be placed in their hands *after* the presentation is over.

Problem Two: Presentations Are Expensive and Work Best with Limited Audiences

If your task is to assure that all 25,000 members of your company understand the new retirement plan, are you likely to use a presentation to accomplish it? The sheer logistical problems make having a presentation—or even a series of them—highly impractical. Assuming yours is a worldwide company, you could summon them from around the globe, pay for transportation, food and lodging, hire a huge convention hall (if you can find one) or a baseball dome (use the scoreboard for the visuals). . . .

You get my point; the project is unthinkable to anyone who cherishes continuity of employment.

Clearly the most efficient way to reach very large and widely dispersed audiences is through the ancient (and still thriving) device of writing. If the stakes are high enough to justify the expense, however, presentations to three or four thousand people will work. Today's audiovisual technology has made reaching huge audiences possible, but the expense is equally huge, especially since the audience is usually being paid to attend.

Presentations in general are expensive. The artwork, photography, and physical setting can be costly, but the audience is usually by far the most expensive element in a presentation. Very often, even a short presentation to a group of corporate officers can cost hundreds of dollars in their salaries alone. Therefore, before deciding to use a presentation to convey information, consider the costs and the logistics. Then ask how your objectives can be accomplished using another medium, such as a report, memo, bulletin, brochure, booklet, procedure, or manual.

The key to these kinds of decisions is asking the question, "What's at stake?" If the stakes are high enough to justify the cost of a presentation, and you would benefit from its special benefits, do it.

Problem Three: The Pace Is Sender-Controlled

In a presentation, the audience has no control over the pace of delivery. Readers, on the other hand, can move at their own speed and can reread difficult passages. Listeners have no such luxury. If the speaker is talking too rapidly, audiences quickly become fatigued and drop out mentally. If the speaker is talking too slowly, audience members begin to use the extra time to think about other things—vital matters that are pressing for attention just below the surface. They take brief mental excursions and return to the presentation without missing anything important. Eventually the compelling nature of their personal matters forces them to return to the presentation too late. Some essential information is lost, and the problem is compounded by a speaker who is dawdling and droning on. The result is the same as with a too rapid delivery—the audience drops out mentally.

Of course, if a speaker is able to tailor the pace of delivery to the needs of the audience, problem three is no longer a problem. Based on my observations of hundreds of business presentations, however, improper pace is a widespread impediment to effective audience communication. Indeed, in some cases, where audience members have sharply diverse backgrounds and widely differing rates of absorption, writing may be a more appropriate method of communication. Most often, however, the cure is to adopt a pace slow enough not to exhaust the less informed and fast enough not to bore the experts in your audience.

The intent of this section is to provide a perspective on audiovisual presentations in contrast with other methods of communication, especially written methods. The purpose is twofold: first, to help you make more informed decisions when choosing methods of organizational and business communications, and second, to point out the strengths and limitations of the presentation. Table 1 is a quick summary of the main points.

Table 1   Advantages and Disadvantages of Audiovisual Communication

Advantages	Disadvantages
— Immediate Feedback	— Impermanence
— Impact	— Impractical for very large audiences
— Control over the communication process	— Expensive
— Less work for the audience	— Pace is controlled by the speaker

HOW FORMAL SHOULD YOUR PRESENTATION BE?

Imagine a spectrum that ranges from the most informal presentation to the most rigorously formal. Here is an example of the informal end of that spectrum: A manager convenes subordinates (let's say five supervisors) to review the past week's production figures and to explain the use of a newly modified production control form.

As an example of the opposite end of the spectrum—the most formal type of presentation—try this: A vice president of research and development must conduct a presentation for the board of directors to justify a new venture for the corporation. The new venture is a controversial, radical departure from the company's core business. It involves new, complex technologies, new marketing strategies, and a business plan that will require expenditures of $75 million. The new venture has the potential to reverse the company's ominously declining sales and profits.

To be successful, the two presentations should be quite different. And since presentations can fail because they are overly formal or too informal, it is useful to understand the reasons and the requirements for more or less formal presentations.

Reasons for a More Formal Presentation

The first and perhaps most important reason that compels a more formal presentation is *the stakes*. The more one may gain or lose, the more formal the presentation is likely to be. Gains or losses can include not only the acceptance or rejection of your proposal, plan, program, or idea but also other factors, such as the gain or loss of budget allocations, space, capital programs, personal status—indeed, the success or failure of presentations can affect careers.

The next factor is *audience disposition*. If the task of a presentation is to persuade an audience that is largely predisposed against the presenter's objectives, the need for a more formal approach increases in proportion to the extent of that antipathy.

The same is true of factor three, *complexity*. The more an audience must struggle to understand difficult material, the more one must use the elements of formal presentations.

Factors four and five are related: *audience size* and the need for *repeat performances*. Other factors being equal, the larger the audience, the more formal the presentation. Usually the need for repeat performances also means reaching a larger audience, the difference being that the total audience is addressed sequentially—one audience at a time. In both cases, it is usually important to ensure that a large group of people reaches uniform understanding or agreement on a subject.

Now you can be a bit more analytical in your view of the two examples of presentations mentioned earlier. Table 2 compares the informal and highly formal presentations using the five factors discussed.

Requirements for a More Formal Presentation

A direct relationship exists between the degree of formality of a presentation and the amount of preparation required to produce it. The more formal the presentation, the more effort should be expended in *preparation*. Preparation means:

- Determining the objective of the presentation.
- Analyzing the audience to determine its knowledge level and, if relevant, its attitudes.
- Developing a strategy.
- Organizing the information to achieve the most effective results.
- Preparing a script that integrates the visual and the auditory messages for maximum clarity, impact, and retention.
- Selecting a visual medium that is appropriate for this audience, this information, this objective, and this degree of formality.
- Carefully considering all the physical factors that can either enhance or frustrate the communication process.

Table 2   Comparing Degrees of Formality

Factor	Informal	Formal
1. Stakes	Weekly review plus introduce change in production control form	Extremely high — major venture — company's future at stake — $75 million program
2. Audience opposition	None likely	Yes, it's a "controversial, radical, departure" — requiring "new marketing strategies"
3. Complexity	No problem	A "new, complex technology" must be dealt with, plus a business plan explained
4. Audience size	Five subordinates	The Board of Directors — presumably not large — but enormously influential
5. Repeat Performances?	No	Probably yes . . . if the plan is accepted, others in the organization will require the information. In fact, the likelihood is that this presentation would be given several times prior to the "final" presentation to the Board of Directors.

- Conducting (if necessary) a dry run to test the expository and persuasive strengths of the presentation as well as the effectiveness of the speaker's delivery.

Every presentation requires some degree of preparation. Even the most informal presentation involves decisions on nearly all the above steps. Sadly, those decisions too often are made randomly and without examination. For example, every presentation has some type of organization. The mere fact that information must be presented sequentially means that the presenter must *decide* on a sequence. It is quite another matter, however, to begin with the realization that organizing information effectively is crucial to an audience's understanding and acceptance of one's material, and then *to use* that realization to decide what information to include, what major and minor themes to use, and in what sequence to array the information and arguments. Remember, a presentation is a *deliberate act*. The elements of preparation are a vital part of that act.

The more formal the presentation becomes, the more emphasis must be placed on effective *delivery*, for audiences tend to view the material being presented as an extension of the presenter. Moreover, the ability to establish rapport with and hold the attention of an audience are directly related to delivery skills.

The remainder of this book will deal with these two subjects: procedures for effective *preparation* and techniques for effective *delivery*. The seven sequential steps in preparing a presentation are:

1. Define your objective.
2. Analyze your audience.
3. Consider your tactics.
4. Organize your information.
5. Create the audio and visual channels.
6. Produce your visuals.
7. Consider the physical factors.

We will explore each step in the sequence of preparation before turning to the eighth and final step: delivering the presentation to an audience.

3

Define Your Objective

In the early 1960s, the expression *terminal behavior* first came into wide use. The term was used to describe how people performed after taking programmed instruction (self-teaching) courses. Terminal behavior was measured by examinations given to a random cross-section of the people who took the programmed instruction courses, and it was expressed statistically. The idea was to measure human behavior in a limited sphere—in this case, the learning of a body of information. Moreover, by measuring terminal behavior, we can gauge the effectiveness of the communication process.

Sounds a bit clinical, you say. Perhaps, but an effective presentation is rooted in the exacting analysis of behavioral objectives.

Every presentation results in some form of terminal behavior by each member of the audience. In many cases, the behavior is obvious. In presentations with immediate objectives, such as the allocation of resources, the adoption of a new program, or the proposed solution to a problem, the reaction of audience members is usually apparent. They either agree, disagree, or fall somewhere between. This reaction is typical of the *persuasive* presentation, in which audience members are asked to decide something and act on that decision in a predictable way.

Many presentations, however, do not have such immediate and explicit goals. Some presentations seem to be purely *expository*, their only purpose being to convey information to the audience. But even these informational presentations will eventually condition the behavior of audience members in some way; the only questions are "How?" and "How far in the future?" For example, a presentation given to describe the function and activities of your organization may be wholly informational in content, but the long-range objective may be to foster a greater appreciation of those activities in order to influence decisions that lie far in the future.

WHY ALL THIS TALK OF BEHAVIOR?

Knowing that every presentation should exist in order to influence the behavior of audience members is crucial because it focuses your energy in the proper channels. The objective, for instance, is not to present yourself well or to show clear, convincing visuals. Those things will be helpful in achieving your objective, but they have nothing to do with audience behavior; they deal with your behavior. In short, the beginning step in a presentation should be an inquiry into its ultimate results.

What is the *objective* of *your* presentation? What do you wish the audience to be aware of, to believe, to *do?* What terminal behavior do you seek? The answers to these questions affect virtually everything you do in preparing and delivering a presentation. The *objective* becomes the touchstone for all the elements of preparation and the reason for making the presentation. (In fact, the inability to state an objective is an excellent reason for *not* having a presentation.)

In other words, once you state your goal in terms of specific audience behavior, everything you do thereafter should focus on achieving that goal. For example, in organizing information, you must decide of all the information you possess on your subject just what should be included. For much of the information the decision is relatively easy. Often, however, there is information that is marginal. In these cases, the answer to the question, *"Do I need this information to accomplish my objective?"* should resolve the problem.

Consider the ending of a presentation. Most presenters treat it as the *ending* place where they stop talking and start answering questions: "Well, that's all I have. Are there any questions?" But if you are concentrating on objectives, the ending becomes your last bid to achieve your goals, and that ending is much more likely to have focus, impact, and persuasiveness than would otherwise be the case.

The whole inquiry into strategy arises out of the knowledge that the presentation is only one element in the larger complex of communications and human interactions, and that achieving the *objective* often requires more than the conducting of a single, brief presentation.

Preparing and delivering an outstanding presentation are never the objectives themselves; rather, they are crucial tactics in achieving the overall objective. Neither is the objective to entertain or amuse, although these tactics, when used with discrimination, may enhance the probability of success in certain situations. The objective lies outside the realm of the presentation itself; it is "audience-centered," not "presenter-centered."

Determining the objective of a presentation is useful in many other ways. The process can:

- Help to define the problem, the issue, or the need that gives rise to the presentation.
- Narrow the scope of the presentation to just the topics necessary to accomplish the goals.
- Help to develop the central theme and the supporting themes, the first steps in organizing the information.
- Provide a means of evaluating and ranking information.
- Help you decide on the appropriate degree of formality.
- Provide a standard of success.

The definition of success in this process is achieving your objective. Defining that objective is important, because it is often easy to lose sight of your goal. When the presentation and its aftermath are memories, the only accomplishment that really matters is that you achieved your objective.

Let's try an example of how to use objectives to plan a presentation.

Assume you have been working on a project for the past six months to determine the effects of airborne factory dust particles on the quality of your product and the health of employees. Your research has uncovered the fact that dust contamination is the direct cause of a 2 percent loss in production yield. Further, a full 60 percent of all customer returns are due to dust particles. The incidence of respiratory problems and related absenteeism is 10 percent higher than equivalent operations in other industries.

You estimate that the installation of dust control equipment would not only improve the working environment for the factory employees, it would save the firm the following amounts annually:

Increase in production yield: $2,000,000
Decrease in customer returns: 300,000
Reduced absenteeism: 700,000

In addition, the improvement in air quality would provide a more comfortable environment, especially for those employees with dust-related allergies.

You now must bring the results of your six-month study to fruition . . . in the form of a presentation to Mr. Bullard, the Vice President of Manufacturing. What is the *objective* of that presentation?

In this case, the objective is easy to determine: Your aim is to convince Mr. Bullard to approve a capital request for $800,000. How do you *use* that objective to plan your presentation?

Begin by asking, *"Of what does Mr. Bullard need to be convinced in order to sign the capital request?"* Let's assume you narrow it down to two items:

1. He needs to be convinced that dust in the factory is a serious problem, requiring prompt control measures.
2. He needs to be confident that your proposed solution is the best one available to him to solve the problem.

Now put yourself in his mind. What kinds of questions are you going to be asking if you are Mr. Bullard and you are seeking assurances that 1 and 2 above are true? Let me suggest a few:

- Is there really a dust problem? What evidence exists to support it?
- What is it costing my operation? Short term? (lower productivity, lower quality, human factors) Longer range? (damaged product reputation, loss of market share, lower profits, legal action?)
- Do my competitors have similar problems?
- If so, what are they doing about it?
- How soon do I need to act on this?
- Are there better ways of dealing with the problem than spending $800,000 for dust control equipment?
- The capital cost is one thing, but what about the ongoing expenses of operating it?
- Is the equipment he's recommending the best for the job? (cost, reliability, reputation of manufacturer, serviceability. What about the competition?)
- What guarantee do I have that this will be an effective solution to the problem?
- How long will installation take?
- What disruptions, if any, will the installation have on production? Any inconveniences or other problems for our employees?
- What is entailed in maintaining and repairing the equipment? Will our employees perform this, or will I have to purchase it from the vendor?
- Does Schmedly (that's you) really know what he's talking about?

It is quite likely that this is not the entire list of questions for which Mr. Bullard will need satisfactory answers, but it's a fair beginning. Your next step will be to arrange the questions in categories (the problem, the equipment, cost factors, etc.) and then to develop the answer to each question. If, by the time you have finished the formal part of your presentation to Mr. Bullard, you have answered 95 percent of his questions, the odds are quite good that you will realize your objective.

You could have approached the presentation in a more traditional way—for example, by giving background on the study that was conducted, who commissioned it and when, who participated in it, how it was conducted, how long it took. But that kind of detailed background information doesn't focus on accomplishing the objective.

Admittedly, the little illustration you just read is a simple example. The objective was straightforward; the "audience" was a single person, and the issues were sharply drawn. But the *technique* it employs is remarkably successful in planning a presentation:

- Determine the objective(s).
- Define the knowledge and beliefs that will produce the terminal behavior you seek from your audience.
- Consider all of the questions, concerns, and counterarguments the audience is likely to have on the way to developing the awareness and confidence they will need to take the action you are seeking.

OBJECTIVES MUST BE REALISTIC

What objectives are realistically attainable given your specific situation and the audience you must reach?

For example, assume you are the Vice President of Personnel in your organization. You are preparing a presentation dealing with the advantages and disadvantages of the four-day workweek for your company. You are convinced that the adoption of the four-day workweek is in the best overall interests of the firm, but you realize that the idea will be greeted with much skepticism and resistance on the part of top management. What should be the *objective* of your presentation to a committee of top executives?

If you decide that your objective will be to seek a consensus to establish the four-day workweek throughout the entire company immediately, your presentation faces virtually certain failure. Part of the process of setting objectives is determining what the logical, practical *next step* can be in the journey toward achieving your ultimate goal. A more realistic objective in this case might be to obtain agreement to organize a steering committee that would set the guidelines for a pilot experiment with one or two departments.

After evaluating the results of this first phase, the decision on whether or not to broaden the scope of the program or return to the status quo could be made by your audience members. In this second case, the presentation is far more likely to meet with success. By setting achievable intermediate goals, your final objective becomes much more attainable.

Objectives . . . lie at the core of effective presentations.

4

Analyze Your Audience

O nce the objective has been determined, the focus turns logically to the audience, because the *audience* must accomplish the objective. If it were within your power to achieve your goal alone, you would not be spending your time preparing a presentation!

To be successful, any communication must be audience centered, whether it be a formal presentation or a notice on a bulletin board. Knowing what sort of terminal behavior you seek from an audience is a beginning. You must also be able to reach that particular audience. In this chapter we will be dealing with building profiles of audiences and the techniques of audience communication.

Presentations appeal to both the intellect and the emotions. True, the themes of most business and technical presentations are based on logical premises, but emotional factors are almost always present. Constructing an audience profile, therefore, is an attempt to determine both the knowledge and attitudes of audience members.

In order to reach (inform and persuade) an audience, you need to know something of what *they* know. You also need to know how they feel about your topic and about you. Lastly, you must use that knowledge both in preparing and in delivering the presentation.

AUDIENCE BACKGROUND

What does your audience know about your subject? You can think about audience background in two ways:

1. What is the *general* level of understanding of your topic?
2. What do specific, key audience members know about your *specific* plan, proposal, design, thesis, program, or idea?

("Key" audience members are those who have a direct bearing on whether or not you achieve your objective.)

The answers to these questions are important, because they dictate one vital element in reaching an audience: *level of detail*.

How much detail must you provide to ensure that your audience can follow your exposition? This is not an easy question to answer, even under the most obvious circumstances. For example, while reading the newspaper one Sunday morning, I strayed from my usual preoccupation with the sports and editorial pages and stumbled onto the following set of instructions on how to produce a chemical reaction:

Flan, New Style

1/2 cup sugar	1 tall can evap. milk
2 eggs	1 can cond. milk
1 egg yolk	1 tsp. vanilla extract

Put sugar in heavy saucepan and heat, stirring until melted to golden syrup. Put in 1 qt. casserole, beat eggs and yolk together, add evap. milk and with rotary beater, beat mixture into cond. milk. Add vanilla and pour into casserole. Set into pan of hot water and bake in 325° oven 1 hour, or until set. Unmold in serving dish and serve warm (not hot). Serves 6.

It was hard to find a place to begin to decipher it. (My greatest culinary achievement is my internationally famous recipe for toast.) I had considerable difficulty with "one egg yolk," not having the remotest idea of how to get the yellow part free from the white stuff. The fact that the recipe later calls for mixing *all* the eggs is still a source of wonderment.

Here is a partial list of the things that perplexed me that Sunday morning:

- Flan, new style (Is there an old style?)
- Cond. milk (Does not compute.)
- Heavy saucepan (What does a saucepan look like, and how can I tell if it's heavy enough?)
- Casserole (Isn't that something with tuna and noodles?)

- Rotary beater (Is there any other kind?)
- Until set (Set for what?)
- Unmold (I give up.)

What you are witnessing is an *audience* problem. The instructions do not provide a sufficient *level of detail* for me to follow them. Of course, the fault lies not with the recipe author in this case. After all, I had no business peeping about in the cooking section. The shorthand descriptions were completely adequate for the intended audience. If the author had to write the recipe for culinary cretins to perform, it would have to contain a vastly greater level of detail:

> "Obtain the yolk of one egg as follows: Crack the egg shell into two halves by tapping it against the rim of a bowl, as shown in figure 1. Separate the yolk from the egg white by slowly pouring the egg white (which is actually not white, but a clear substance) into one of the two halves. . . ."

Of course, the entire recipe would have required perhaps 10 times the space, and what is far worse, the usual readers would have been colossally bored by the unwanted level of detail.

Technical presentations often pose more problems of audience analysis than do purely business presentations. Occasionally, some audience members have little knowledge of the technology and no awareness of the specific application, design, or technical concept being discussed. The same audience can include people with advanced knowledge of your subject. The challenge in these cases (and in most cases) is to provide a level of detail that will not lose the former or test the patience of the latter too severely.

How often is this a problem? In practice, audiences with huge discrepancies in background are rare. But such disparities exist, and when they do occur, you must be prepared to cope with it. Here are some suggestions for coping:

- If you must err, let it always be on the side of *overcommunication*.
- It is best to tailor the level of detail to the least knowledgeable member of the audience *whose understanding is essential to the accomplishment of your objective*.
- It is better to provide more supporting background than less. The well informed members of your audience are likely to be patient (and even feel magnanimous) if you explain the need for more supporting detail because of the wide diversity of backgrounds in the audience. Providing *less* supporting detail than is needed will exclude some members of your audience from participation. Those whom you exclude will become bored and preoccupied or frustrated and angry, depending on their involvement in your subject and their motivation for attending.

- If you face a gulf in understanding so wide that you literally have two audiences, consider giving *two* presentations. The first can be a basic exposition for people needing the special background. The second can then be given to both audiences. Another tactic is to give two presentations in which audience members are chosen by their familiarity with the subject. Of course, the level of detail would be tailored in each case to the audience selected.

Even though such formidably disparate audiences are rare, the task of reaching even a normal audience is seldom easy and should never be taken for granted. Communicating with an audience is much like walking atop a fence. In choosing the proper level of detail, you must constantly strive to keep in balance. Fall one way and you elicit impatience or boredom; fall the other and you produce confusion, frustration, and often anger.

AUDIENCE ATTITUDES

Not all of your challenges are related to what your audience knows. Often the obstacles to the terminal behavior you seek lie in the attitudes of audience members. In fact, the more persuasive the presentation must be (as opposed to expository or information giving), the more crucial becomes the need to analyze the attitudes of key audience members.

How does your audience *feel* about your idea, proposal, plan, scheme, design, conclusion, notion, theory, solution? Audiences respond to presentations both intellectually and emotionally. We appeal to their sense of logic on the one hand to convince them of the correctness of our arguments. We also appeal (depending on the situation) to their sense of pride, fear, isolation, indignation, compassion, gregariousness, and a host of other emotions to convince them of the persuasiveness of our arguments.

How much persuading must you do? The answer lies in the attitudes of the people who come into the room to experience your presentation. Specifically, what are their attitudes (preconceptions, biases, prejudices, feelings) toward your *objective* and—often as important—what are their attitudes toward *you?* The more antipathy your proposal faces, the more you must work to win over the audience. Where one argument might suffice, three are needed to win converts. One example may not be enough to make a point. Moreover, it's not just the number of arguments that makes the difference, it's the soundness—the invincibility—of the arguments that must be forged carefully.

If you face a personal credibility problem with an audience, you have an excellent chance of overcoming it, first, by following the suggestions above on *level of detail* and the *number and power of your arguments*. (Some audience members may be surprised to learn that you are much more capable than they had imagined!) You must constantly work to establish your own stature by knowing your subject thoroughly and by being in charge of your material as well as the presentation itself. But in addition, you must de-emphasize yourself in the content of the presentation. Avoid the personal pronoun. Focus on the ideas and their impact, not their source. Wherever possible call on the testimony of others—influential, respected, familiar figures who support your position. Lastly, when appropriate, attribute the idea to others as well as (or instead of) yourself. Much merit exists in the old saying that there is no limit to what you can accomplish when you don't care who gets the credit. It almost never happens, but the worst possible audience you can face is one in which all four elements of your analysis yield problems:

1. The audience possesses very little *general* understanding of your subject.
2. They have no technical knowledge of your *specific* proposal.
3. Your audience is, in general, opposed to your proposal.
4. Most of them are convinced that you possess the brains of a cucumber!

As the great conductor Arturo Toscanini once said to an orchestra and chorus about to begin Beethoven's majestic and difficult Ninth Symphony: *"Coraggio."*

OBTAINING THE INFORMATION

How do I get all this information on audience backgrounds and attitudes?

List the members of the audience and note those who will influence the achieving of your objective. All members of your audience are important, because they influence each other in the questions and discussions that take place. But the group of *key* members can *individually* thwart your purpose. They warrant closer attention.

You can make certain general (careful, the word is *general*) inferences based on the organization to which an audience member belongs. (How would someone from manufacturing be likely to react to this plan?) Other general inferences may be made based on the status or rank of the individual in the organization—especially as it relates to the other members of your audience. Look at job titles; they can tell you much about each audience member's technical background and the awareness of your specific subject each is likely to have.

In addition to these passive observations, you may choose to take active steps to obtain information about your audience. Consider contacting individuals and asking them directly what they know and how they and others feel about elements of your presentation. Use your communications network to learn from others who will not necessarily be attending, but may be well informed. Incidentally, this is not to be viewed as a clandestine process. You are gathering information that will be used to help tailor your communication to the needs of a target group, a productive, if not commendable, practice. If the stakes and the situation warrant it, for example, consider preparing and sending a *questionnaire* to audience members.

Usually, the important point is not how you obtain the information, but that you *do* obtain it.

COMMUNICATING WITH AN AUDIENCE

Having gathered the information you need about your audience, it is now time to make use of it. Let us examine the process by which we reach an audience.

A good place to begin is with a working definition of human communication: *Communication is the transference of thought through physical signals.*

You can have as many thoughts as you wish, but you can communicate none of them without creating a physical signal that can be sensed and interpreted by at least one other human being.

These signals fall into two categories: verbal and nonverbal. Verbal signals involve the use of words, written or spoken. Nonverbal signals involve everything else we do that conveys information to others. When we speak, for example, perhaps 5 or 10 percent of the "message" derived by our listeners comes from the words alone. The rest comes from how we say the words (pace, intonation, inflections, stresses, volume, animation levels), facial expressions, posture, mannerisms, eye contact (or lack of it), gestures, and our appearance in general.

This suggests that, in contrast with writing, effective speaking requires an awareness that a multiplicity of information channels is at work. (This is *not* intended to devalue writing, which presents its own special communications challenges.) The abundance of information channels also explains in part why business people and technical professionals usually prefer face-to-face communication to memos and reports. The mixture of signals is richer and more suited to their need to assess, evaluate, interpret.

What happens when we communicate with others? Let's examine the process.

It begins with an idea or a collection of thoughts in the mind of a person who needs to share that information with someone else. The communicator *transforms* the idea into a cluster of physical signals. In face-to-face communication this typically consists of speech sounds accompanied by facial expressions and other body movements, all of which comprise "the message,"

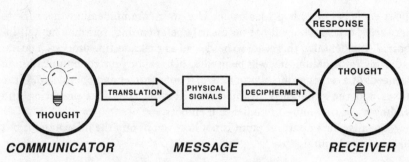

Figure 1   The Communication Process

which is directed at one or more persons. The communicator creates the physical signals and *offers them up* for interpretation by the receiver.

The receiver must now decipher the signals and *create* meaning. It is crucial to the communication process to recognize that every member of your audience creates his or her *own* meaning, and that in every instance, that newly created meaning is different from your original thought. As Figure 1 shows, thoughts, or "meanings," can exist only in people. The message—the physical signals offered up by someone wishing to share thought—does not possess meaning. The message is the collection of clues that allows us to find meaning within ourselves.

Ultimately, communication is a two-way process. It becomes complete when the original receiver responds by creating a new cluster of signals to be interpreted in turn by the initiator. And it is at this first moment of response that most of our problems with communication begin.

The culprit in communications failures is often false assumption. The sender of the message assumes that his meaning was faithfully transmitted. The receiver, moreover, assumes that his or her interpretation of the message is what the sender intended. Neither of them is aware that communication has not occurred. The receiver *responds* in ways that lead the sender to assume the message was correctly understood. The sender in turn neglects to *test* if the audience interpreted the message correctly. Both are condemned to continue the process unaware of their mutual dilemma. The false assumption that we have communicated is the easiest and most natural to make. Don't be fooled.

COMMUNICATION IS SHARING

You can communicate with people only on the basis of what you share with them. Indeed, the word *communication* comes from the Latin word *communes*, "to share or to make common." Thus, the success of any communication is directly related to your ability to use what you possess in common with your audience. In practical terms, this means considering all you have learned of what your audience knows and doesn't know about your subject as well as what attitudes your audience possesses and using that information to help you think and feel as they do! It means carefully choosing a level of detail that will allow all audience members to participate fully. It means avoiding words likely to be unfamiliar to audience members as well as defining unfamiliar terms whose use is necessary. In the last analysis, effective communication means the ability to suspend your own ego temporarily and *become* your audience.

Either by instinct or by design, every good communicator develops the ability to construct a mental image of a typical audience member and then uses that image to test every word, every sentence, every image, every idea. In presentations, the craft of audience centeredness goes beyond considerations of audience backgrounds and attitudes. It pervades the entire process: organization, script preparation, design of the visual content, physical factors, delivery, and even handling questions. In the long run, the more audience-centered you become, the more successful you are likely to be.

The keys to reaching an audience are three:

1. Know your audience's background.
2. Know your audience's attitudes.
3. Become your audience. Talk their language. Use the proper level of detail and weight of argument to inform and persuade them.

THE MAKING OF A COMMUNICATOR

In some quarters the ability to communicate effectively is regarded as a black art. Those who regard it with less awe view communications skill as just one of many management and professional tools. Becoming a really effective communicator does, however, require certain attitudes and frames of mind. Here are some examples.

Desire

All of the most impressive skills in the world are of limited use if you don't *want to communicate* above nearly everything else. That statement has a certain ring of truth. You probably agree with this notion immediately. But agreeing in principle is easy. Doing it is not.

First, you must be prepared to give up some of your individuality. The things that make you special—your education, training and experience—can become obstacles to communication. Let's say you are a scientist presenting your findings to a group of business associates who have little or no background in your technical field. You can speak like a "scientist" if you wish, but you will lose much of your audience. Using the scientific terms and the jargon you are so comfortable with will confuse, bore, and even *alienate* audience members.

But giving up the special language of your profession and making an effort to introduce new terminology to your audience doesn't allow you to "sound" like a scientist (engineer, economist, lawyer, nurse). This is a sacrifice that few people are willing to make, partly because those professional credentials took years of hard work and sacrifice to earn, and partly because one's profession provides status and is a cherished part of one's identity.

Good communicators desire to communicate so greatly, they are willing to make the sacrifice.

Work

Communicating with others is hard work, largely because all communication is based on *sharing*. As you know, you can communicate with others only by using what you possess in common with them. Think of how much more effort is required when you consciously restrict yourself to using only language that you are confident your audience shares with you. Think of the added work you must do to choose a level of detail that will neither inundate nor bore your audience. Consider the burden placed on you to constantly test your terminology against the measuring stick of what you *suspect* your audience knows. For many, the very act of being audience-centered is cumbersome and laborious.

Good communicators are prepared to do the work.

Humility

Pride is an enemy of communication, especially the kind of pride that prevents you from asking questions when you don't fully understand what someone is trying to communicate. T. S. Eliot tells us, "In order to arrive at what you do not know, you must go by a way which is the way of ignorance."

The first step in the learning process is the acceptance of one's ignorance and the willingness to admit to it if necessary. Pride, of course, can prevent such admissions. Good communicators, however, tend to be lifelong learners. They *want* to understand. They put pride aside and become engaged when they miss an important point or idea.

Good communicators are not reluctant to say, "I don't understand" or "Would you explain that further?"

Desire, work, humility—three important characteristics that help us transcend ourselves to become effective communicators.

5

Consider Your Tactics

A presentation is an intense concentration on a subject for a brief period, a deliberate act involving the programming of an audio as well as a visual channel. But in a larger sense, a successful presentation extends beyond the walls of the room in which the presentation takes place and beyond the brief time in which the sounds and the images occur. Why? Because a presentation involves the behavior of the participants.

It is shortsighted to expect that the presentation alone will accomplish your objective. At this stage, you must ask: What options are available to me and what actions can I take *beyond the presentation itself* to help accomplish my objective? These actions are collectively called the *tactics of a presentation*. I will touch on several kinds of tactics, but the choices and the options are endless. It is essential to realize the ranges of choices and actions that are available. Then you must choose and you must act. Otherwise, the realm of tactics is abandoned to the vagaries of chance.

HOW MANY PRESENTATIONS?

Let us begin our examination of tactical options with a simple question: Are you more likely to accomplish your objective with a single presentation, or with a series of them, each one building toward the final adoption, acceptance, and approval of your proposal?

31

For example, several years ago it became my task to propose a system of technical information for a new plant manufacturing a highly sophisticated technical product. The plant manager had three subordinates, each with major operational responsibilities. We could easily have formulated a final plan for the plant and presented it to the four executives in one heart-stopping roll of the dice. Instead, we chose to present our proposal to *one* of the three subordinates. After receiving that manager's comments and suggestions and incorporating them in the proposal, we repeated the presentation and feedback process for the second, and then the third member of the plant manager's staff. At last, we were ready for "The Presentation" before the plant manager and the three senior managers. The final version was a ritual of review, minor revisions, and confirmation on the part of the audience. The three operating managers were not only familiar with the proposal, they had *contributed* to it.

Similarly, when it it becomes necessary to build a widespread consensus in an organization, it is a common practice to use a *series* of presentations as a kind of traveling forum to elicit comment, to test and sharpen the proposal, and to win supporters. A side benefit of this process is that the presentation itself as well as the delivery improve with repetition.

Part of your tactical analysis should be to determine how many presentations are necessary and to whom those presentations should be given.

TIMING

When should you conduct the presentation? Often the scheduling of a presentation is beyond your control. In fact, usually you do not have sufficient time to prepare completely. But to the extent you can control the time of the presentation, you should do so with these two thoughts in mind:

- Always allow yourself enough time to prepare properly; the results of hasty and incomplete preparation are always apparent in the end product.
- Time the presentation for the maximum impact. Avoid times when other events may cause key members of your audience to be absent.

WHO SHOULD ATTEND?

If the presentation is informational, who needs the information? If the objective is to work on a problem, what human resources will you need to understand its complexities and put forth the effort to help solve it? If the presentation deals with assigning responsibilities, who are the people who will be given the responsibilities and who are empowered to assign them?

On rare occasions, you may wish to exclude someone from the presentation. It is conceivable that someone can be so intractably opposed to your objective that his or her presence will frustrate it. Another example is the individual who constantly dominates a problem-solving session to the extent that everyone else's ideas are stifled. It may not always be possible to exclude such problem people from your audience, but when it is, *do it!* You may choose to send a secondary group of people a summary of the presentation, even including copies of your visuals. Your "problem person," of course, would be so informed.

In practice, however, it is seldom that easy, because accomplishing your objective usually requires the support and cooperation of such people. In any event, you can never exclude anyone whose participation is necessary to accomplishing your objective. Fortunately, there are other alternatives.

PRELIMINARY ENCOUNTERS

Audience members usually fall into one or more of the following classes:

- *Positional*—This person is attending principally because of the position he or she holds in the organization. Often the approval (or the absence of disapproval) of such a person is crucial to achieving the objective.
- *Representational*—This audience member attends to represent a part of the organization and hence the point of view of that group (department, division). The representational member is charged with advancing and protecting the interests of the group.
- *Sacrificial*—Occasionally your audience will include one or more members who will have to give up something, such as control, desirable space, position, a cherished program, staff, or operating funds, if your objective is to be achieved. Clearly, this kind of audience member is one of the most difficult to persuade and motivate.
- *Responsible*—This audience member will be asked to do something, such as carry out a program, achieve a goal, assume more responsibility, or conduct a study. This person's reaction to the presentation will be directly linked to how the new responsibility will be perceived. A challenging and rewarding project is likely to be viewed much more favorably than an increase in work load without additional resources, for example.

Most business presentations deal with either bringing about or coping with change. When you are planning such a presentation, consider these questions: Who will be asked to change? Who will be asked to sacrifice or to assume more responsibility or simply to take on more work? Whose support will you need? Who will be opposed to your objective?

These and similar questions point to the importance of meeting with such people *before* the presentation. Preliminary meetings with individuals or small groups can help you discover the sources of support or opposition to your objective. They can also help you learn or confirm the roles that key audience members will play. The ideal tactic is to exchange information and seek either participation or acceptance. Very often, 30 minutes over coffee cups can ensure the success of months of work.

Bear in mind that resolving the inevitable problems of change is best begun at the individual level in preference to the group level. The inhibitions of individuals in group processes as well as the momentum that can occur in groups make it difficult to deal with deep-seated resistance, biases, or objections of individual members. The value of meeting with pivotal members of your audience *before* the presentation should always be considered when difficulties lie in the path of accomplishing your objective.

OVERCOMING OBSTACLES TO ACHIEVING YOUR GOAL

Adversaries

My belief has always been that people who are *open* in their opposition to your plan, proposal, or idea are to be numbered among your friends. Spending time with such "adversaries" will help uncover flaws in your arguments, weaknesses in your case, chinks in your armor. By all means work with such adversaries, not just to convert them, but also to use their thinking to modify and sharpen your presentation.

Very often one can encounter resistance to proposals in organizations from some individuals based not so much on the facts as much as on the fact that their opinion was not sought. Their resentment at not being consulted can be turned into implacable opposition. Indeed, the vast majority of opposition to new ideas or plans within organizations is due to not being consulted before the decision was made. Most people need to know that their ideas were at least considered. They may be unhappy that those ideas were not adopted, but they will reluctantly accept the outcome because they at least had a measure of participation. You may not entirely convert a potential adversary to your point of view, but by seeking his or her opinion, you will at least not have created an adversary by omission.

Negative Information

Tactically, one of the worst decisions you can make is to omit negative information. If you include only the information *supporting* your objective, you will most surely lose credibility with members of your audience, especially if their questions open up whole areas of inquiry that you have chosen to ignore in the presentation. To succeed, your presentation must be objective.

But how does one deal with negative information? To begin, it is important to view your presentation as a lawyer does a case. What are the most telling arguments? What are the pivotal issues? What are the weaknesses in the case? What questions can be expected from the audience? What hurdles must be cleared to achieve the objective?

Next, for practical purposes, divide the negative information into two categories:

1. Points that are potentially damaging to your case.
2. Secondary concerns, questions, and objections.

Information in the first category *must* be included in the presentation. Not doing so will result in an obviously one-sided presentation and a loss of credibility. Audience members are forced to conclude that you either intentionally deluded them or you were inept in your analysis and misled them unintentionally. Neither reaction is the one you want. The proper tactic is to demonstrate that the negative information has been carefully considered and, when weighed against all other factors and brought into correct perspective, it does not alter your conclusions or recommendations.

Information in the second category need not be included in the presentation. But if it is not, be prepared to answer questions comprehensively and convincingly. You must answer in a way that tells your audience that the point has been carefully considered and, for the reasons you provide, has been rejected or reduced to a minor factor.

THE TACTICAL FRAME OF MIND

It is impossible to imagine every situation in which tactics serve as the vital element in achieving your objective. But one fact is certain: It is naïve to assume that the presentation alone—no matter how well put together and convincingly delivered—will carry the day. Part of a comprehensive preparation should always involve being aware of and exploring *all* the opportunities that exist in order to overcome obstacles and to ensure success.

6

Organize Your Information

WHY BOTHER?

Most people do not like to spend time organizing the information they will use in a presentation. They give a variety of reasons:

"The press of time doesn't permit it."
"It's too much trouble."
"The return isn't worth the effort."
"I know exactly what I want to say; it's all organized in my head."
"Orchestrating every detail robs the presentation of spontaneity."
"It won't make that much difference anyway."

The curious fact, however, is that *every* presentation has some kind of organization—intentional or not—because every presentation requires three elements:

1. *Inclusion*—From all the information you know about your subject you must choose only those facts, arguments, and details you deem necessary to achieve your objective.
2. *Subordination*—The choice of the *major topics* you will use to cover the material and all the *supporting topics*.

3. *Sequence*—The choice of a coherent *order* in which to convey the information.

Notice that each element requires making choices. Since every presentation involves inclusion, subordination, and sequence, *every presentation* is the product of such choices. The important question is, will you make these choices consciously and carefully, or will you decide to improvise? Your best course is to consider your choices and then make them deliberately. The alternative is . . . well, let me illustrate.

THE ZOOMIE PACKAGING COMPANY

Imagine that your chief packaging engineer has the task of evaluating a new packaging machine for your company. After an investigation, the findings and recommendations are to be presented to the manufacturing management committee, perhaps in the following way.

Good morning, ladies and gentlemen. My trip to Zoomie Packaging Machinery Corporation was most enlightening. I arrived at Trenton at about 3:48 p.m. last Tuesday, the twelfth. Mr. Zoomie was most helpful and informative. His chief engineer, Max Able, met me at the airport. He seemed most capable technically. Max recommended the Globe Hotel--an excellent choice, although their food didn't measure up to their service.

Next morning--the thirteenth--I saw the new Model Z-2300, automatic, in-line packaging system. This is an outstanding, state-of-the-art design. The use of digital logic controls plus high-speed overwrapping make the Z-2300 the most advanced packaging machine available in the industry. Max explained that it took three years and $18 million to develop it.

The Zoomie people were most gracious and accommodating, answering all my questions completely and candidly. I was most impressed by Max Able and his design team, who felt they were able to adapt the Z-2300 to our specific packaging application.

Conservative estimates indicate that the Zoomie Z-2300 will increase packaging capacity by 18 percent. That evening in my hotel room, I calculated that our present five machines can be replaced by four Zoomies with a labor reduction of 20 percent.

I am convinced that the reliability record of the Zoomie Z-2300 will exceed that of our present machines. Max Able assured me that four machines can be delivered and installed at our facility

within 180 days. Zoomie's record of support and customer service
is the envy of the industry.

Of course, because the Zoomie Z-2300 is a high-speed,
positive-action packaging system means that about 35 percent of
our ice cream cones will be crushed in packaging. Unfortunately,
the system is wholly inappropriate for our products, even though
the Zoomie technology is most impressive.

We can hope that the Zoomie people will develop a packaging
machine for fragile goods such as our number five sugar cones. The
graciousness and cooperation of the people at Zoomie impressed me
greatly. They are an excellent firm to do business with. My return
flight on the morning of the fourteenth was uneventful.

WHAT IS THE PROBLEM?

What is wrong with this presentation? The obvious answer is, "It is poorly
organized." But that is too easy. The deeper problem—in fact, the most common problem with defective organization—is that it is *self-centered* and not
audience-centered.

If you review the Zoomie presentation, your first impression might be
one of undisciplined rambling. The impression is not quite correct. The presentation does have a loose organization. It is a rough chronology of the trip
to Trenton. Woven into the trip story with all its irrelevancies are bits of analysis of the Z-2300. The elements are all given from the *presenter's point of
view*. From the audience's point of view, the most important information
comes near the end of the presentation and, even then, almost as an after-
thought.

Effective organization always begins with the question: "What does my
audience need?" In the Zoomie case, the answer comes in three parts:

1. Do you recommend that we substitute the Zoomie Z-2300 for our
   present packaging machine?
2. Why? (Or why not?)
3. What additional details are worth knowing?

In our make-believe case, these three classes of information look like
this:

1. *Must know*—I do not recommend that we substitute the Zoomie
   Z-2300 for our present packaging machines.
2. *Important to know*—The Zoomie Z-2300 is a high-speed, positive
   action packaging machine that will crush about 35 percent of our ice
   cream cones.

3. *Nice to know*—Details that were not provided in the original presentation. Here are some examples:

- Does Zoomie have another model that can meet our needs?
- Can Zoomie modify one of their packaging systems to handle our sugar cones?
- Is Zoomie willing to develop a high-speed ice cream cone packaging system? If so, how much would it cost and how long would it take?
- Are any other packaging systems manufacturers worth considering? If so, who? If not, why not?

It is useful to think of the three classes of information as a target, as you see in Figure 2.

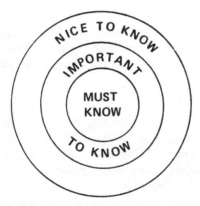

Figure 2   Three Classes of Information

A well-organized presentation is *audience-centered*. It begins with the bull's-eye and works outward. Thus, the audience gets the most needed information immediately, followed by supporting facts and arguments. Highlights and significant details come last. Information outside the third ring does not belong in the presentation (the food and service at the Globe Hotel notwithstanding).

Time should have an effect on organization. How much time do you have to cover your material? It is conceivable that time could limit your presentation to the bull's-eye only. Many presentations consist of the two inner rings only, because of time constraints.

Organization is the craft of selecting and arraying information and arguments in a way that satisfies the needs of your audience in the time they have to receive it.

The best way to *record* that organization is with an outline.

ORGANIZING THE BEGINNING

The cliché about the persistence of first impressions surely applies to presentations. A feeble or confusing beginning usually creates a lasting impression, one that may be impossible to overcome. How, then should you begin?

Once again, begin with the needs of your audience. Here is a list of what every audience member has a right to know in the first minute or two of a presentation.

Who Are You?

If the audience does not know you, introduce yourself. It may also be necessary to provide a *brief* note about your background to help establish your credibility in the subject you plan to present. Of course, if the audience does know you, don't waste time with introductions. If they know you but are unfamiliar with your competence in the subject of the presentation, give them a sentence or two about yourself. Be careful not to overdo it. A presenter who begins with a lengthy, self-serving autobiography can alienate an audience.

What Are You Up To?

What is the subject of your presentation? What is its *purpose?* What are you trying to accomplish? What is the problem, if any? From the audience's viewpoint, answer the question, "Why should I sit through this presentation?" Many presenters feel that informing the audience of the presentation's purpose at the outset is a strategic blunder ...

"If they know what I'm up to, they'll leave the room before I can get started." Or "If I tell them everything in the beginning, all the suspense will be gone."

Your audience has not come to attend a play. They are there to accomplish some productive purpose. Keeping them in suspense is not a wise tactic. Neither is it helpful to withhold a controversial purpose you may be trying to accomplish. When the audience finally does have the trap sprung on them, they are likely to feel manipulated. By all means come to the point in the first minute. If someone *does* leave the room, it is likely that the purpose you have described does not involve the departing person, and you have saved his or her valuable time.

What Is the Scope of the Presentation?

What subject territory will you cover? Remember, not every aspect of a subject will always be covered. For example, a presentation might cover the cost/benefit analysis of a capital investment but, because of insufficient data, not deal with the extensive environmental questions. In such a case, the scope statement should point out what the presentation *will not* cover. Not to do so is to invite unnecessary and perhaps embarrassing questions, interruptions, and digressions.

What Are the Criteria?

In some presentations, the objective requires that the audience accept conclusions and support recommendations based on the analysis and the arguments that you present. In this type of presentation, the audience must know the rules of the game before it begins. The criteria form the basis for making the key judgments that will decide the outcome—for example, cost, efficiency, morale, effect on product quality, technical feasibility, and/or profitability—the list is endless. Spell out the criteria, or decisive factors, for your presentation in the first minute.

What Do You Expect of Me?

Every audience member deserves to know what his or her role will be. Put yourself in the shoes of your audience. Am I expected merely to absorb information for my own use, or will I be expected to use it to help solve a problem? Will I be expected to make a decision? Commit resources? Comment on the feasibility of the proposed design? Tackle a new assignment? Convey the information to others in the organization? Knowing one's role at the outset of a presentation helps an audience member relate to the material properly. Moreover, the terminal behavior you expect at the conclusion becomes immediately apparent.

What's in It for Me?

One of the great deterrents to listening is the perception that no benefit is to be gained. How will this presentation *benefit* your audience? What organizational goal will be advanced or even gained? How will individual members of your audience be better equipped to perform their tasks? How will their work lives or status be enhanced? Granted, not all presentations are easy to cast in the light of audience benefit, but always look for it. Use your imagination. And let your audience know at the beginning of the presentation.

People tend to remember what they experience at the beginnings and the ends of things. The lesson is simple: Do not waste beginnings and endings; use them to accomplish your objective.

THE MIDDLE

With the preliminaries out of the way, the middle, or body, of the presentation can now assume its role of informing and persuading the audience. Think of a presentation as a sandwich: The beginning and the end come from a bakery; the *type* of sandwich you eat is determined by what goes in the middle.

As mentioned at the start of this chapter, organizing information calls for three types of decisions or choices:

- *Inclusion*—What information should go into the presentation?
- *Subordination*—What are the major themes and supporting themes?
- *Sequence*—What is the order in which the information will be presented?

The result of all this choosing is an *outline,* which will become your road map when you prepare the script for your presentation. Many methods can help you create that road map. Later, this chapter will cover several patterns of organization. For the moment, however, let's concentrate on the simple idea of *themes.*

Every presentation should have a *main theme.* The main theme is the nucleus, the central idea or assertion on which the entire presentation is built. Often, the best way to begin working on the middle of the presentation is to state its main theme:

We should install dust control equipment in the production area.

This technique is helpful not only because it distills the essence of a presentation, but also because it provides a statement of your objective (in this case, to obtain approval to spend $800,000 for dust control equipment).

The next question is, "Why?"

We should install dust control equipment in the production area because:

1. It will reduce quality control production losses by 22 percent (net annual savings: $275,000).
2. It will reduce customer returns by nearly 30 percent (net annual savings: $300,000).
3. It will create a more healthful environment for production workers.
4. Installation of the equipment will not disrupt production or affect quality.
5. Improved quality will ultimately boost sales.

By placing yourself in the shoes of your audience and asking "why," you can evolve the supporting themes, or *subthemes.* Each subtheme (1 through 5) can in turn be organized by asking, "Can you prove it?" and then by listing the points necessary to convince your audience of the validity of each sub-theme.

The following section provides a more extended example of the use of main theme and subthemes to organize information for a presentation.

G&T COMPANY, FAIRLAWN PARK

You are the Community Affairs Manager for Goode & True Company, a highly successful manufacturer of scientific instruments. A big part of your current assignment is to help G&T acquire a 60-acre parcel of land in neighboring Oaktown's Fairlawn Park.

Fairlawn Park has long been one of Oaktown's most conspicuous assets. The 300-acre park is studded with lovely old trees and small ponds. However, Oaktown, because of a pressing need to broaden its tax base, has voted to sell a little used corner of the park to a suitable occupant for $20 million.

G&T Company is one of several organizations interested in this highly desirable site. Among the competitors are a rubber company, a highrise apartment developer, a heavy machinery manufacturer, a shopping center developer, and an agent representing about a dozen small businesses, such as distributors, garages, and plastic novelty manufacturers.

Because G&T is such a successful business, the company needs land for expansion of its instrument manufacturing facilities in the immediate future. The Fairlawn Park site is nearly ideal for this purpose in every respect. Accordingly, G&T has hired famous architect, Frank Lloyd Rong, to develop an excellent architectural plan for the site, including attractive buildings that preserve and take advantage of the site's natural beauty. The site development plan also gives careful attention to local traffic patterns. An architectural model and several architect's renderings of the buildings are available.

Goode and True has 5,700 employees. An unusually high percentage are professional people, and most of the remainder manufacture complex scientific instruments. Over the 25 years since its beginnings as a highly creative company, G&T has established an excellent reputation, not only as a thriving and resourceful business, but also as a forward-looking organization. G&T employees have traditionally become involved in the community affairs of nearby Elmwood, where G&T has its present offices and plant (a complex of very attractive buildings). The company has always been active in Elmwood civic affairs and has made many contributions to worthy local causes.

G&T has an outstanding management team whose efforts over the years have met with continuous growth of sales and earnings. The company has one of the strongest financial positions in industry.

Virtually all G&T's manufacturing operations are considered light industry. No significant amounts of hazardous waste materials, pollutants, noise, or odors are produced. The company is keenly conscious of its public appearance and has an outstanding record of campus-type site development as well as maintenance and improvement of its properties.

Personnel and pay policies equal or exceed those of the leading manufacturing firms in the Oaktown area. G&T employees are not unionized and are quite loyal to the company. Employee turnover is exceptionally low. G&T plans to add about 500 people to its payroll over the next three years, mostly for its expanding manufacturing operations.

In addition to meeting the $20 million purchase price, G&T plans to spend $60 to $80 million developing the Fairlawn Park site over the next 10 years, as its worldwide operations grow.

Oaktown is a community of 35,000 residents with many small and even marginal businesses, but not many major industries. Lately, the town has been straining to meet the needs for educational and municipal services from its hard-pressed tax base.

Apart from some road construction and street lighting, G&T does not expect to have a heavy demand for local services. The company pays for such things as waste disposal and snow plowing. G&T's locating in Oaktown will not significantly increase the school population, and the overall impact on the town's economy appears excellent.

Oaktown's seven Town Council members, who range in age from 43 to 68 years, are, of course, aware of the town's economic problems. All are longtime Oaktown residents; all have the best interests of the town uppermost in mind. Three of the seven are owners of small Oaktown businesses; the remaining four are professional men and women.

Your task is to convince the Oaktown Town Council that G&T is the best candidate for the Fairlawn site, because it is the Town Council that will recommend an occupant to the town in their upcoming report. The next town meeting will probably adopt their recommendation.

Organizing the G&T Presentation

Notice that the information in the G&T story is random—without focus, direction or purpose—as is the case in real situations.

Step One: A Main Theme

Goode & True Company is a highly desirable choice for the Fairlawn Park site, both as a company and as a developer and occupant of the site.

Step Two: A Basic Topic Outline

This topic outline is typical of how a first draft might appear.

  I. Introduction
 II. G&T Company (general)
     A. As an enterprise (what kind of company)
     B. As an organization (what kind of people to do business with)
     C. As a neighbor and community member
     D. As a developer and owner of property
III. G&T as an occupant of Fairlawn (specific)
     A. Details of the development plan
     B. Impact on the immediate environment
     C. Impact of G&T on the economy of Oaktown
 IV. Summary/discussion

Step Three: An Expanded Outline

The final task is to expand the subthemes of the topic outline into an *expanded outline* that will serve as the road map for preparing the script. Notice that the expanded outline contains some information that was not given originally. This is a delightful by-product of the process of organizing information to achieve an objective.

  I. G&T as an enterprise
     A. Brief chronology: emphasis on G&T dynamism, resourcefulness, inventiveness, products, reputation, position in the industry, growth prospects
     B. Financial strength
        1. Consistent growth of sales and profits over many years
        2. G&T's assets and net worth: continuous growth

      3. Current operating and financial statements provide information on the magnitude of G&T operations and profitability

      4. Future prospects are for continued growth and prosperity

   C. Current situation: on threshold of new expansion

      1. G&T's expansion plans

      2. Suitability of Oaktown and Fairlawn Park site

II. G&T as an organization

   A. Corporate philosophy: forward-looking, human dignity, individuality, progressive attitudes, quality of management, reputation

   B. Excellent employee relations

      1. Pay and benefits: among leaders in industry

      2. Low employee turnover; a "good place to work"

      3. Employees have a voice; do not feel the need for union representation

      4. Growth of company due largely to creativity, perseverance, and loyalty of its employees

   C. Type of employees: professionals, specialists, highly skilled production workers

   D. G&T has an excellent reputation as an employer

III. G&T as a neighbor and community member

   A. Relations with other communities have been outstanding

      1. History of involvement in community affairs

      2. Past contributions of time, talent, and dollars to communities

   B. G&T is a responsible neighbor

      1. Campus-type vs. heavy industry

      2. Absence of pollution problems—G&T recognizes its environmental responsibilities

      3. G&T assumes responsibility for nearly all its own needs—waste disposal, snow plowing, security, etc.

      4. The company is convinced that the abutters' property values will increase as a result of G&T's presence

IV. G&T as a developer and owner of property

   A. G&T has the technical competence to excel in the task of land development

      1. It uses the best architectural talents available

      2. Its past architectural accomplishments indicate the importance the company places on its site development skills

   B. G&T has a reputation not only for initial quality, but also for continuing concern: upkeep, maintenance, and improvement are equally important to our employees and to our neighbors

   C. The advantages of dealing with a single developer, rather than several, are important to a community (control, efficiency, simplicity, etc.)

V. Our plan for the development of the Fairlawn Park site
  A. Final appearance of the site: showing of architect's model—include all aspects of the plan
  B. Types and quality of construction
    1. Buildings: density, use
    2. Roads: access, egress
    3. Parking facilities
    4. Landscaping: use of natural features
  C. Impact on immediate environment
    1. Favorable impact on remainder of park and abutters
    2. Absence of environmental abuse or depletion
    3. Impact on area traffic flow
  D. Schedule and cost
    1. When (after selection) construction would begin; how quickly it would progress; when it would conclude (mention temporary inconvenience during construction)
    2. G&T Company's projected future investment in the site
    3. Possible long-range expansion at Fairlawn
VI. Economic impact: benefits vs. costs
  A. Benefits to Oaktown
    1. Tax contribution
      a. History of taxes paid to other communities
      b. Estimated annual taxes G&T would pay
    2. Favorable effects on local business and services
    3. G&T employment potential
      a. Long-range, steady growth
      b. Wide diversity of customers
  B. Costs to Oaktown are minimal, especially compared to other types of development (e.g., residential)
    1. Nearly all costs of development borne by G&T
       Exceptions:
      a. Some road construction
      b. Street lights
    2. Continuing costs to Oaktown few and small
      a. Negligible impact on schools
      b. Small (or no) requirement for local services such as roads, utilities, police and fire services, snow removal, waste collection
  C. In sum: many economic benefits, few economic costs
VII. Conclusion
  A. Summarize by briefly stating the benefits to Oaktown derived from G&T's acquiring the Fairlawn Park site; stress G&T as a business

    enterprise, organization, community member, developer and owner of property
B. Extend to Town Council members and any guests an invitation to tour the G&T facilities at Elmwood

The G&T expanded outline reflects decisions carefully made to bring purpose and emphasis to a collection of random information. But, of course, that outline is not the only way to organize the presentation. You probably have your own suggestions for improvement, and that makes sense. Each of us views information from different perspectives and with different values. It is possible that a major point for one person is not worth air time for someone else. Differences in how we perceive the audience, differences in objectives—even differences in the time available for the presentation—will affect the outline. Organizing information, like communication itself, is not a science; it is a craft.

Next we will explore some of the important patterns of organization and examine the differences between telling and selling.

EXPOSITION OR PERSUASION?

It is useful to think of presentations as falling into two classes:

- *Expository*—A presentation in which the objective is simply to impart information to an audience.
- *Persuasive*—A presentation in which the objective requires persuading the audience to support a program or take a course of action. This type of presentation relies to a large extent on logical arguments.

Of course, pure examples of either class are rare. Almost every presentation contains a *mixture* of information and argument. But separating the expository and persuasive elements can help you recognize the special patterns of organization each uses. Knowing the patterns will allow you to be consistent in how you use them.

EXPOSITORY PATTERNS

When the objective is mostly to give the audience information, then your presentation can use one of the following organizational patterns.

Chronology

This pattern involves relating a series of events in time sequence. The pattern is simple to use, but be careful to include only events that are important to the total exposition. The most common error is the omission of an important event. Another problem with chronology is providing the exact level of detail to suit your audience's needs.

Analysis

From the Greek *ana lien,* to break asunder, analysis is the dividing of your subject into parts and explaining each part in turn. Analysis is often used for technical presentations in which one must discuss parts, assemblies, systems, and phases. Analysis is a divide-and-conquer method that can work well.

Classification

The counterpart of analysis, classification is the collecting of items with certain common qualities into categories. Classification is a potent tool. It brings logic and order to a presentation. It simplifies explanations and makes them easier for an audience to grasp and retain. Employees, for example, can be classified any number of ways, such as male/female, hourly-paid/weekly-paid/monthly-paid, production/professional/clerical/trades/managerial. Management employees can be further subclassified as supervisory/middle management/executive/officer.

Cause and Effect

As you might expect, cause and effect is a mainstay of business and technical presentations. We are always explaining the likely consequences of our actions or the probable outcome of technical design decisions. Cause and effect has a dual nature. We can start with causes and explain the effects they produce, or start with effects and trace back to their causes. An example of the latter is the "how-we-got-into-this-fix" presentation.

Question and Answer

What is the first thing the audience needs to know? The second? The third? Question and answer consists of posing each question and then answering it. Consider using Q&A organization whenever your presentation requires explaining a limited body of information to your audience. The Q&A technique requires that you project yourself into the minds of your audience, because you must ask *the* most appropriate questions at the precise times that your audience would ask them. You must clearly and completely answer each question. Lastly, you must answer *every* relevant question your audience is likely to ask about your topic.

Expository presentations are by no means rare, and the higher one's perch in the organization tree the greater the need becomes for information. A corporation president, for example, needs to have a huge assortment of information on many subjects in order to make good decisions. Usually the expository presentation is triggered by that need, which comes in the form of questions, such as:

1. What is the problem with X, and what are we doing about it?
2. What do this year's capital expenditures look like?
3. How is the new product coming along?
4. Are we competitive with our employee benefits?
5. What is our research and development organization working on?

Very often, the question itself can set the organizational pattern of the presentation. The first question above can be answered by a presentation that:

• Provides a detailed description of the problem;
• Reviews the available solutions;
• Explains why you chose the solution you did;
• Provides a current situation report; and
• Projects when the "problem" will be solved.

Classification can help answer question two. Capital expenditures can be grouped by either those for equipment or for facilities. Expenditures for equipment can, for example, be further subclassified into equipment for manufacturing, research, product development, data processing, environmental protection, and departmental operations.

Question three requires a progress report. The scope of that report depends on who is giving the presentation. For example, if the product design and development group is reporting, the presentation will typically consist of technical and operational problems overcome, problems being solved, and prospects for the timely availability of the new product. If, on the other hand, the progress report will be presented by the corporate program manager for the new product, the scope broadens to include the status of the business plan, product development, manufacturing scale-up, marketing progress, and overall schedule.

Question four calls for a presentation with a simple organization—a benefit-by-benefit *comparison* between us and other specific companies (or a community average).

For question five (which is trickier because it is a general question), classification might work best. Organize the presentation around *categories* of work (hardware, software) or *disciplines* (optical, electronic, mechanical, chemical). Another approach is *organizational*. Explain the major work in progress based on the departments or project teams performing it.

In each case, the organizational pattern reflects the original question that prompted the presentation. If the question is vague, do not hesitate to get a more specific version. You could be organizing an answer to the wrong question!

PERSUASIVE PATTERNS: LOGIC

Most business presentations require persuasion. Objectives usually involve convincing other people to fund a program, approve an expenditure, adopt a new policy, prevent an action from being carried out, or even maintain the status quo. The basic difference is that of advocacy. In a persuasive presentation, you must organize the information into logical *arguments*. Arguments are the reasons we provide to convince others that our conclusions are true. The audience should be aware of your position from the outset, and you should expect your arguments to be questioned and challenged. But your *logic* need never be disputed. The rules of logic evolved many centuries ago, and the patterns of logical argument are as compelling today as they were in Aristotle's time. Here is a brief overview of the major patterns of logical argument.

Deduction

With *deduction*, you begin the argument with a statement (major premise) that every audience member must accept as true and then proceed to build a conclusion, using that beginning statement as a foundation. For example:

- *Major premise*—All customer returns have been for incorrect wiring of the tuning circuit.
- *Minor premise*—Line five does all of the wiring of the tuning circuit.
- *Conclusion*—Therefore, production line five has caused all customer returns

This logical process is called a *syllogism*. Remember that when you use the syllogism, your audience *must* accept your major premise. If the statement isn't indisputable, you cannot use this deductive pattern. Be especially careful of seemingly universal (but mushy) truths, such as, "All employees are seeking self-fulfillment." In deduction, the major premise must withstand every test of truth; if it does not, the whole structure of the argument crumbles and falls.

To be correct, a syllogism must satisfy two conditions. The major and minor premises must be *true* and the reasoning must be *valid*. Here, for example, is a syllogism in which the three statements are all false yet the reasoning is valid:

All Martians are wombats.
Mr. Wilson, head of quality control, is a Martian.
Therefore, Mr. Wilson is a wombat.

Here is another syllogism; this one contains an error in reasoning:

All our employees are brilliant people.
All geniuses are brilliant people.
Therefore, all our employees are geniuses.

In this case, brilliant people contains two classes, our employees and geniuses. But no logical connection has been made between our employees and geniuses. The conclusion is invalid.

Finally, here is a syllogism in which the premises are both false and the conclusion is true:

All roses are animals.
My cat is a rose.
Therefore, my cat is an animal.

In all three cases, the deductive reasoning is unsatisfactory.

One last point: in ordinary conversation, parts of the syllogism are often missing; they are *implied*. This does not make them incorrect. For example:

Poorly designed products will not survive in the marketplace.
Our Model 20 Excalibrator will not survive in the marketplace.

In the above case, the minor premise (Our Model 20 Excalibrator is a poorly designed product.) was implied.

Induction

In the inductive pattern, an *accumulation* of individual facts builds to a *general* conclusion, for example:

1. Of our 15 products, only the Modulator is unprofitable.
2. The Modulator is a complex, outdated design being overwhelmed in the market by less expensive, more reliable imports.
3. Customer returns of Modulators is 9 percent, substantially higher than any other of our products.
4. We have enough Modulators in inventory for 10 months' sales.
5. We need Modulator production workers to help make other products that are backordered.

Therefore, we should stop producing Modulators as quickly as possible.

This accumulation of facts supports the conclusion and allows the audience to make the so-called *inductive leap*. Before making that leap, however, the audience must be convinced that the overwhelming weight of facts supports that conclusion and *only that conclusion.* The more instances we can show as evidence, the more likely it is that the audience will accept the probable truth of the conclusion. The above example is unusual in that every fact supports the conclusion. In real situations, the facts are hardly ever so one-sided, and you must prove that your conclusions *on balance* are correct.

Analogy

Analogy is an extended comparison of the similarities of two basically different things. Analogy can describe and explain as well as persuade. For example, one may explain the human heart by comparing it to a pump and describing the operation of the chambers and the valves in mechanical terms. But when you use analogy to predict or to prove, you are using analogy as an argument. In an analogical argument, you must find as many similarities as you can between two different things. Each point of similarity serves to strengthen the argument. Your goal is to draw enough relevant points of resemblance to convince your audience of the high *probability* that other, not yet *revealed,* or *less obvious* points of comparison exist as well.

For example, imagine that your company is considering the development of a new product. You give a presentation that draws an analogy between that new product and a notorious marketing misstep, the Edsel automobile. You describe the similarities in market targets, market conditions and trends, economic climates, product similarities, competitive products, and so forth. If your analogy convinces your audience that they are about to approve the development of the next Edsel, I submit it should be a reasonably effective argument. Remember, in order to be effective, the analogy must contain points of agreement (or matches) that are *clear-cut, relevant, and numerous.*

Elimination

This persuasive pattern calls for listing all the alternatives, then disposing of them one by one until the audience is left with either the best course of action or the most likely cause of a problem.

This approach may sound simple, but elimination has its pitfalls. To begin with, you must list *every* reasonable alternative (or cause, if you are isolating the source of a problem). Few things can be as devastating as being asked by your audience if you had included a viable alternative that you have not considered, let alone analyzed. Your unpalatable choices are to debate the new alternative on the spot or to admit that you had not considered the alternative in your analysis.

Next, you must slay all the dragons but one, which is not always easy to do. Sometimes dragons get resurrected by uncooperative audiences or, alas, your surviving dragon has a fatal flaw to be pointed out by an especially astute and helpful audience member.

Despite its pitfalls, elimination is a powerful technique for organizing persuasive presentations. Done correctly, it can be elegantly compelling, even memorable.

REBUTTAL

Occasionally your presentation may call for refuting the arguments of others—arguments that have been expressed or that you have anticipated. Here are the major forms of rebuttal, should you have need for them.

First, you may attack the *facts* of the argument. Your refutation must include proof of the correct facts.

Second, you may accept the facts of the argument, but attack what they *prove*. This refutation is based on the use of logic. You must substitute more convincing proof.

Third, you may accept the facts and the proof, but show that the wrong *inference* has been drawn from both.

Here are examples of the three common ways to rebut an argument.

- *Argument*—The overwhelming majority of the 40 supervisors we surveyed were unhappy with the new performance review system. In fact, 80 percent of them called the system "a nightmare." Those supervisors are just the tip of the iceberg. It is clear that the system is not working.
- *Rebuttal 1* (denial of facts and counter assertion)—The so-called survey referred to was a preliminary, informal opinion of 32 supervisors on first hearing of the plan. At the time, the plan was in its proposal stage. As you see in the chronology I am submitting, the opinion was given four months before the plan was even introduced.
- *Rebuttal 2* (denial of proof)—The survey did take place, but to conclude the system is not working is a hasty generalization. One cannot assert that the preliminary opinion of 32 supervisors (who are likely to be disenchanted with *any* performance review system) applies to the 1,500 supervisors, 300 managers, and 10,000 people who have been using the system successfully for over two years.
- *Rebuttal 3* (denial of inference)—In the survey, 32 supervisors did express unhappiness with the new system. However, the problem is *not* with the system but with the supervisors who, in this case, are not sufficiently trained to use the new system properly.

Fourth, you may answer the argument with a *retort*, which is a sharp counterthrust, often using the words of the argument itself. For example, a retort to the argument that "our budget cannot afford this project" might be, "I am convinced that in our long-range interest we cannot afford *not* to undertake this project!"

Fifth, you may show that the argument is contradictory, inconsequential, trivial, or even ludicrous. The formal name for this refutation is *reductio ad absurdum* (reducing the argument to an absurdity).

A final word: Remember that rebuttal always involves attacking *arguments,* never the *people* who propose them. Personal attacks not only violate the rules of argument, they can antagonize your audience.

SOME CONCLUDING THOUGHTS ABOUT PERSUASION: EMOTIONS

In the previous section, we discussed the patterns of organization that apply to persuasive organizations. Persuasion is an arrangement of facts that appeals largely to our sense of logic. It would be shortsighted, however, not to mention that it is not always pure logic that persuades us.

We are creatures of emotion as well as intellect. Sometimes the most logical argument imaginable will not convince an audience that your cause or your course is right. Why? Because it doesn't "feel" right. Audiences must be moved to action in spite of all your reasoning. Presentations, after all, usually propose change. Most people don't like change; they find it unsettling and threatening.

The list of emotional factors that can affect the outcome of a presentation is as long as human experience itself. As we touch on a few of the most important of these nonlogical factors, remember to be aware of them not just as potential obstructions, but also as powerful allies in the process of persuasion.

Fear

An emotion with an undeservedly poor reputation, fear can be a healthy motivator. We use other words to describe this emotion, of course. We are "concerned" that profits are slumping, for example, or a bit "apprehensive" about the reliability of the latest design. Whatever the terminology, if the situation warrants it, we can either *act* out of fear or, curiously, be *paralyzed* by it.

Gain

The desire for gain is often the force that moves entire organizations as well as individuals. It is naïve to assume that audience members do not view any proposal in the light of personal as well as organizational gain. As a rule, the higher one's position, the more one's goals become identified with those of the organization.

Incidentally, it is a mistake to always clothe the desire for gain with the cloak of greed. Lincoln wanted the power of the American presidency; Gandhi wanted to gain independence for India; Saint Francis of Assisi wanted to establish a religious order. Wanting to gain an increased share of the toothpaste market is by no means so lofty a goal, but neither is it to be ridiculed.

The other side of the gain equation is the *avoidance of loss*. Once having achieved something, we tend to want to hold on to it. Loss avoidance, in fact, is one of the most common themes of business presentations.

The Herd Instinct

Most of us see ourselves as independent thinkers. But organizations engage mostly in group activities, and being out of step can be intensely uncomfortable. Examples:

> Mr. Bullard, our car is the only one on the market without front-wheel disk brakes.
> Our employees are the only ones in the industry without medical coverage.

Testimonial

Testimonials can have a strong, persuasive influence in business presentations. You may not care which athlete eats what breakfast cereal, but you may be influenced by the judgments, or even the opinions, of someone whose proven expertise and credibility on the subject at hand are outstanding. Of course, citing a prominent, highly placed, and influential member of your organization as an enthusiastic supporter of your proposal is mere name dropping—a shabby practice that practically no one condones, but almost everyone employs.

Other Emotional Factors

The range of human emotions produces a wide variety of responses in communication. We all share a sense of pride and have a measure of competitiveness and compassion. Most of us enjoy a challenge, take risks, and seek recognition and acceptance. In the last analysis, these seemingly nonlogical factors can often tip the balance scales one way or the other. A successful presenter is always aware of their presence and is always aware that logic alone does not rule the human will. If it did, Sir Edmund Hillary would never have climbed Mount Everest.

THE ENDING

The most important key to a presentation's ending is *do not waste it.* We tend to remember the beginnings and endings of things. The ending of a presentation represents an *opportunity,* not just the point when you stop talking. Yet, an all-too-common practice is to end the presentation with, "Well, that's all I have. Any questions?"

How you construct the ending depends largely on the subject and your objective. In a highly expository presentation, it is important to summarize each section as you go along. The conclusion can be a brief summary of the main points and some suggestions on how to get more information or how to apply the newly acquired knowledge. In a persuasive presentation, consider the ending as your last chance to achieve your objective. Use it to summarize your chief arguments or conclusions. If appropriate, give an especially telling example of the problem or stress the consequences of not adopting your proposal. And by all means include a hook.

A *hook* is the next logical, feasible step in the process of reaching your ultimate objective. Remember, the presentation is never an end in itself; it is a vehicle for achieving that end. What happens *after* the presentation is usually more important than the presentation itself. A hook can take an infinite variety of forms, including the request to approve a proposal, purchase, or program; establish a steering committee; agree to attend a follow-up meeting; sanction a report; approve further study; or agree to have your presentation given to another group. The closing section of a presentation should contain such a hook. *You* should provide it. If the next step is not obvious, create a logical follow-up. Be inventive.

Ask yourself, "What are the four or five main points that I want my audience to remember a week after the presentation is over?" Then use whatever techniques you can to highlight and focus audience attention on those points.

Each presentation has but one ending; don't squander it.

OUTLINING TECHNIQUES

Try preparing your outline on 3-by-5-inch index cards. This will afford you much more flexibility than using the traditional sheets of paper. The method is especially helpful in organizing large presentations. Begin by writing the main theme and all the supporting themes on a single card (use a 5-by-7-inch card if you need more space). Next, write each supporting theme on a separate card (see Figure 3).

Each supporting theme (S.T.) is a *major topic* of your presentation. Next, work on the subtopics under each major topic. This time, list each subtopic at the top of the card, then jot down the supportive items for each sub-

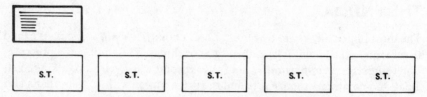

Figure 3 Main Theme and Supporting Themes

topic. The first draft of the outline should look something like the format shown in Figure 4.

You can now look at the entire organizational plan of the presentation and make changes painlessly; thus:

- *Inclusion*—Eliminate cards and add new ones to fill gaps in the flow.
- *Subordination*—Raise a subtopic card to the status of a major topic. Each supporting statement or argument then becomes a subtopic and gets written on a new card.
- *Sequence*—You can change the order of the subtopics for greater impact by simply moving individual cards, or you can change the sequence of major topics by shifting the vertical rows of cards.

Once you are satisfied with the outline, *number* the cards in proper sequence and gather them up. The information on the cards can then be transcribed onto paper either for review by other people and/or for your own use in preparing a script.

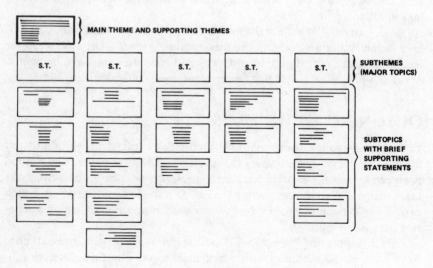

Figure 4 Final Outline

Another technique for organizing your information involves the personal computer. Computer software is available that allows you to enter your thoughts at random, then arrange them in coherent, logical headings and subheadings. All the changes with 3-by-5-inch cards described above can be made electronically. You may have as many headings and levels of subheadings as you wish. You can move or copy any part of your outline, add paragraphs of text, if you wish, and when finished, you can print your outline. One software product will allow you to print word charts from your outline.

Use whatever method works best for you, but by all means don't fail to organize your information. Good organization gives unity, coherence, and focus to your presentation. Good organization helps your audience to understand your ideas and remember your main points long after they have left the room.

7

Create the Audio and the Visual Channels

An audiovisual presentation, remember, is a two-channel form of communication, a series of spoken words and images designed to accomplish a predetermined objective. The more carefully you *plan* those sounds and images, the more likely the presentation will succeed in its purpose.

BEGIN WITH A SCRIPT?

By preparing a script, you commit your plan to paper. A common mistake is thinking of a presentation only as slides or visuals. As soon as we discover that we must give a presentation, many of us begin rummaging through our files (mental and metal), looking for old visuals we can use again—or at least visual ideas we can resurrect in new clothes. Once we have accumulated enough visuals to fill the allotted time, we are ready for the presentation.

The opposite approach is to write out the complete speech portion of the presentation and then go back and try to find the best way to illustrate it. This method at least has a planned audio channel, but it is still not as effective as planning both audio and visual channels simultaneously.

Think of a script as a kind of program sheet that details what the audience will hear and see from the beginning to the end of your presentation. A script is the translation of *ideas* into words and images.

Strangely enough, one of the best reasons for preparing a script is that it liberates you from the dependence on words; it frees you to explain your ideas in your *own spontaneous words*. You will never have to engage in the deadly, boring practice of reading to an audience, or trying to read from cue cards or notes. More on this point a bit later.

Figure 5 shows a convenient and widely used format for preparing a script. Rule an 8¹/₂-by-11-inch sheet of paper into two columns as shown.

The column labeled *audio* should be wider than the *visual* column because more space is needed to write what the audience will hear than is needed to describe what it will see. This two-column format forces you to think in two channels. While you are writing the audio portion of the message, you must also create the visual information that will best illustrate, explain, reinforce, highlight, or amplify the audio message.

The basic unit of a script is called a *frame*. A frame consists of all the vocal and visual information available to the audience during the projection of one slide or visual. In the sample script, notice that horizontal lines are used to separate the frames. Also notice that when the visual consists of just words, the words themselves are used in the visual column of the script. The same would be true of a simple table. Usually, pictures (photographic images and line drawings), complex tables, charts, graphs, diagrams, schematics, and the like are not duplicated on the script. There isn't enough room on the paper. Instead, you enter a description of the visual and explain the points you wish to make with it. For example, "Bar chart showing sales per employee and total bonus dollars paid over the past 10 years."

How long should a frame be? The easiest answer is, "As long as necessary to make the points required." Think of the frame as the equivalent of the paragraph in writing. Like the paragraph, the frame should fully develop a *single idea*. It is important to make a distinction here. Most advertising, marketing, or motivational presentations have short average frame spans. Typical frame durations run from less than one second up to 10 seconds. In business and technical presentations, the frame durations are much longer because the emphasis is on exposition and carefully structured argument rather than creating a mood, engendering a spirit, or conveying a series of impressions. If you are giving a business or technical presentation, be alert for *extremes*. If you are changing visuals every few seconds, something is wrong. Either you are not developing each idea fully, or you are fragmenting your ideas over too many visuals. Conversely, if a visual is on the screen for much more than two to three minutes, the ideas probably should be spread over two or more visuals.

AUDIO	VISUAL
1. Purpose of today's meeting is not to tell each of you what your salary grade is, but to give you an overview of the Company's New Salary Program.	1. Our new Salary Program . . . an overview
2. Here's what we'll cover . . . First, a brief background; why did we need a new salary plan? How was it designed? Next, a description of the new plan, followed by an explanation of how it operates. Then, I'll do my best to answer any questions you may have.	2. Agenda: —Background —Description of the plan —How the plan operates —Discussion/Questions
3. To begin with, the old salary system had several inadequacies. It lived a shadowy existence. It was never corporately administered. It was vague and not understood. No method existed for evaluating jobs, and this led to a noticeable lack of consistency among divisions. These problems caused a growing awareness of the need to review and formalize a salary plan.	3. Background: —Inadequacies of the old plan —Not a formal company system —Vague - not understood —No provision for evaluating jobs —No consistency
4. We needed a system whose structure would truly reflect the value of the jobs — when compared with each other and with the outside world. We needed a system everyone could easily understand. We also needed the methods to apply it uniformly. So much for defining the needs — how then, do we fulfill them?	4. Needed: A salary program that is . . . —Consistent - internally —Competitive - externally —Easily understood —Uniformly administered

Figure 5　A Sample Script

By working in frames, you build both the audio and the visual channels concurrently. However, it is not possible concurrently to describe how to do both. Each must be described in turn. The next section will describe how to prepare the audio channel; the following section will cover the range of visuals available to you and explain the techniques for creating effective (and avoiding ineffective) visuals. It is important to bear in mind that the best practice is to create the audio and visual channels *simultaneously*.

CREATING THE AUDIO CHANNEL

A Good Script Communicates

How many English languages exist today? If you think there is just one, you probably haven't heard two molecular biologists discussing the chemical bonds of two protein molecules, or two computer specialists discussing the intricacies of a ballistics tracking program, or a group of investment analysts exchanging opinions on the latest technical developments in market trends. Moreover, special languages are not solely the property of highly trained professionals. We all use them when we discuss not only our jobs but our special interests, hobbies, or activities. When CB (citizen's band) radio fans "read the mail," they listen to radio chatter without transmitting themselves. "Low profile clinchers (tires) with high-pressure tubes and prestas (valves)" are common expressions to a serious cyclist. In Boston, an automobile traffic reporter is creating his own humorous traffic-jam language with such terms as "ramp cramp," "lane sprain," "grumper-to-grumper traffic," and, my favorite, "gawker blocker" (one who impedes traffic by slowing down to stare at an accident). The profusion of special languages is endless.

A special language uses English as a base and *jargon* to convey the special, exclusive meanings. Jargon is not a negative word, although some dictionaries are beginning to define jargon as "any unintelligible language." On the contrary, jargon is simply the special language of a profession, activity, or occupation. Jargon saves time and will always be with us. The potential problem with jargon is its exclusivity. It is a language for *insiders*.

Communication requires breaching the walls that separate people. The word communication itself derives from the Latin *communes,* to *share* or to *make common.* We can communicate with each other only based on what we *share.* You can communicate with an audience *only by using what you possess in common with that audience.*

The language of communication is simple and familiar. It makes no attempt to impress others with ponderous and learned terms and phrases. One of the most important lessons that all good communicators learn is, *impress people with your ideas, not your words.*

No matter how careful we are, however, we all eventually make the false assumption that we are communicating with an audience. Recently, when explaining to a group of executives how jargon saves words for insiders, I used the following example:

Jargon: Is a 1939D BU Jefferson really worth $60.00?

Plain English: Is a Jefferson Series five-cent coin, minted in 1939 at the Denver Mint, and which has never been circulated and is in bright and unmarked condition, really worth $60.00?

I explained that the insiders—in this case, the numismatists—could communicate much more efficiently using jargon. Then came the humbling event we all need to keep our perspective: One member of the audience asked me, "What is a numismatist?"

For communicating via the audio channel of your presentation, bear in mind these simple rules as you prepare your script:

- Avoid the *unnecessary* use of jargon. Use a language familiar to your audience.
- If you must use unfamiliar terms, *define* them as you introduce them.
- Be especially wary of *acronyms* and *abbreviations*.

Acronyms are words formed by the initial letter or letters of a compound term. SCUBA, for example, is an acronym formed from Self-Contained Underwater Breathing Apparatus. VLSI, on the other hand, is an abbreviation for Very Large Scale Integration, a term from the world of computer chips (microelectronics). If your audience is unfamiliar with the terminology, you can't use it to communicate without first helping them to understand it.

- Be concerned with *level of detail*. How much supportive and amplifying information does your audience need? Too little will be confusing and annoying, too much will be tedious. If you err, let it be on the side of overcommunication. It is better to ask some audience members to put up with more detail than they need in order to prevent others from getting lost and becoming angry. Yes, audience members who can't keep up tend to feel they have been excluded and often become angry.
- Never keep an audience in suspense. Come to the point. Explain your objectives. Suspense is wonderful for detective stories, but it usually irritates an audience of business or technical people.
- Never emphasize the differences between you and your audience; always deal in the similarities. (If you were giving a speech to the Daughters of the American Revolution, you would probably not begin with: "As a life-long, left-wing liberal Democrat, I'd like to explain my views on welfare.")

Other important aspects of the audio channel include style, pace, balance, unity, and emphasis.

The Importance of Style

Always be aware that you are writing a speech. Your speech should sound like *you* do when you speak naturally. Use simple, familiar words. Don't be afraid to be yourself. If the audio channel of your presentation sounds like a written report, at least two bad things will happen. First, you will need to memorize all the fancy language. That's diabolically difficult for most of us. Second, if you cannot memorize it, you will have to read it. That's doubly deadly, first, because the overly formal language puts audiences to sleep, and second, because you should *never read anything* to an audience; it bores them to distraction. A good way to avoid this trap is to dictate your words (following your outline, of course) and then have the recording transcribed into written form, preferably with a word processor to make changes easier. You can then edit the written version, polishing the text and eliminating any confusing or ambiguous passages.

Style means the way *you* express yourself: your manner, your words, not those of Winston Churchill or Richard Burton, but the essential you. One key to successful presentations is simply to be yourself, but be as good as you can be.

Be aware of the *tone* of your words. It is possible unintentionally to communicate an enormous range of impressions to an audience. One's words can seem sarcastic, aloof, paternalistic, grave, condescending, academic, pedantic, or too chummy, to cite just a few of the possibilities. The tone may also be neutral. The important thing is to avoid extremes and to be certain that the tone of your words is appropriate to your subject, to your relationship with that specific audience, and to the situation.

How to Sound Uncertain, Tentative, Vague, and Imprecise

You may have lined up the facts and have the weight of the arguments on your side, but you may still not convince your audience because of your words and how you say them. The problem falls into three categories: weasel words, overqualification, and an unconvincing delivery style. Let's look at weasel words and overqualification now, because they relate to your script. We will examine the elements of delivery style later.

Weasel Words

Imagine that you are the first human to attempt a parachute jump. As you are about to step out of the airplane the inventor assures you, "We've tested it *rather* carefully and I'm *reasonably* sure it *should* work perfectly well." Now go ahead, jump.

Weasel words fall into two categories. The first type—words such as *might, could, perhaps*—erode the *certainty* of your statement: "The product could be available by autumn." The second type blurs the *exactness* of a quantity or of timing: "Most of the project will be completed before long."

Here's a partial list of words to help you sound uncertain:

could	I suspect	probability	unsure
I assume	likely	probable	usually
I believe	may	probably	very likely
I expect	maybe	quite likely	very possible
I feel	might	quite possibly	very possibly
I guess	normally	quite probably	very probably
I hope	perhaps	seemingly	very sure
I imagine	possibility	should	very surely
in all likelihood	possible	somehow	would
I presume	possibly	supposedly	
I suppose	presumably	uncertain	

"When can I have it?" you ask. Well, we're substantially finished with the job. You should have it *soon . . . very soon . . .* in a week *or so . . . as soon as possible*. You'll have it *before too long*.

Next, let's look at weasel words that hedge on amounts, quantities, or times. This too is just a partial list, but it will at least help you get started in confusing, misleading, and frustrating your audience.

a bit	great amount	or so (in a day or so)
a fair amount	greatly	pretty much
a few	guesstimate	pretty often
a great deal	in a while	pretty seldom
a little	largely	pretty soon
a lot	lots	prompt
about	lots and lots	promptly
almost	many	quick
appreciably	more or less	quickly
approximately	most	quite a bit
around	mostly	quite a little
as soon as possible	much	quite a lot
before too long	much of	quite a while
considerable	nearly	quite often
considerably	nominal	quite soon
essentially	normal	rather
estimated	normally	reasonable
few	not a great deal	reasonably
frequent	not much	relatively
frequently	not too much	repeatedly
give or take	often	right away

roughly	the majority of	very great
several	timely	very little
somewhat	unusual	very many
soon	unusually	very much
speedy	usual	very often
substantial	usually	very soon
substantially	very few	without delay

The point is not that you must avoid these words and phrases at all costs and under any conditions. (Although some of them are always worth avoiding, for example, "most" will always be tighter than "the majority of.") In many instances you can't give an exact amount or time. In technical and business presentations, the audience is looking for the most exact information available. If you use these weasel words, you are signaling your audience that you, for whatever reason, don't know a more exact amount than ". . . *a great deal* of our margins have been eroded by the *increased* cost of components." How much of the margins? How much has the cost of components increased?

If your choice of words is *unnecessarily* imprecise or tentative, your entire presentation strikes the audience as wishy washy, and you may be perceived as uncertain and vague.

Choose language that is assertive and be as precise as possible in conveying amounts, times, and frequencies. Your first choice should be to consider giving an actual number or date. The substitution of an adjective or adverb should be a considered and deliberate choice. For example, when my wife asks me when I intend to mow the lawn, I usually say, "As soon as I can get to it, dear." I would never say, "At two this afternoon." Life, after all, is full of uncertainties.

Overqualification

We don't often make unqualified statements, such as, "Methanol will replace gasoline for use in automobiles." We are not utterly certain and need to hedge. Thus, "Methanol will *probably* replace gasoline in passenger vehicles *by the year 2000.*" Two qualifiers: Our old friend and distinguished weasel word, "probably," is back, along with a phrase that provides a time limit for the prediction.

The term "probably" (and words like it—may, could, possibly, likely, might) introduces the element of chance. In statistics the "probability" that an event will happen can range from zero (i.e., it will *never* happen) to one (utter certainty that it will happen). In statistics we can express probabilities with mathematical exactitude. Words are far less obliging. It "more than likely" will happen, "most certainly," "extremely likely." By introducing the element of probability we weaken our statements. *Any* qualifier robs a statement of finality, conviction, and often clarity as well.

Some of the weasel words—especially those dealing with probability—are used as qualifiers. But qualifiers are a much broader class. For example, "All our production problems have been solved." How about "*Essentially* all our production problems have been solved." (How many problems are still unsolved?) "Our cough medication is 100 percent effective." "Our cough medication, *in most cases*, is 100 percent effective." (How often is it less than 100 percent effective?)

When we are unsure of a prediction, or can't make an unconditional statement, we need to use qualifiers. (Try to remember the last time you heard a weather forecaster say, "It will rain today.") The problem that creeps up on us is we *overdo* it. We get too cautious. Academics, scientists, and economists are especially prone to hedging their public utterances. The sad result of all that caution and hedging is that nothing substantive ever gets said.

The process of overqualification is almost endless. One can limit and restrict the meaning of statements to the point of absurdity. Notice how the following example starts with an unqualified statement then proceeds to qualify it beyond all recognition.

1. Speech preceded writing.
2. Primitive people learned to speak before they learned to write.
3. Primitive humans probably learned to speak before they learned to write.
4. Although definitive proof is lacking, it is probably not unreasonable to assume that primitive people learned to speak before they evolved the more abstract and difficult technique of writing.
5. Granting the obvious absence of definitive empirical proof, it is nonetheless reasonably plausible to hypothesize that, in most cases, primitive humans learned to speak before they evolved the more abstract and difficult technique of writing.
6. Although nothing exists that can be even remotely construed as incontrovertibly conclusive evidence, the postulate that in their evolutionary journey up from the Stone Age, humans communicated their thoughts to others in their species orally long before they developed the more difficult technique of representing their thoughts with graphic symbols can in no sense be considered unreasonable, let alone trivial or speculative.

Let me, if I may, just conclude by suggesting that it is quite probably a bit less than a good idea to use too many qualifiers in your presentation (in most cases).

As you prepare your script, strive for the the most convincing, unqualified, and uncluttered way to say your ideas. Do not let an uncertain, tentative style rob your presentation of its forcefulness.

Humor

The tone of a presentation can be humorous. Indeed, there is a persistent belief that *every* presentation must begin and end with a joke. A joke or humorous anecdote puts everyone at ease and gets the attention of the audience. It tends to help the speaker relax. Humor also helps to establish a rapport with the audience at the beginning of a presentation. Use humor when it is appropriate, but also be aware of several pitfalls.

If you use humor, it should be funny to *every* member of your audience. This is not easy to do. Our tastes and sensitivities to humor vary widely. Of course, you *already* have ruled out ethnic, sexist, and bawdy humor. Beyond that be sensitive to the possible reactions of everyone. For example:

"Apart from that, did you enjoy the play, Mrs. Lincoln?"

Your first reaction to that one-liner might be hearty laughter. Your second reaction could be a tinge of remorse. Perhaps to some people it is far from amusing because to them it trivializes one of the most tragic moments in American history. Another example: I have often wondered how many of the people who suffered the horrors of the Nazi prison camps could enjoy the television program "Hogan's Heroes" several years ago. Would the pompous and easily deceived *kommandant* and the lovable, bungling camp guard recall images of real characters from the past?

When writing a humorous tone in your presentation, remember these four rules:

Rule One: Humor should be universal. Everyone should enjoy it.

Rule Two: Do not be a stand-up comic. If your script contains one gag after another, your audience may be rolling on the floor with laughter, but they will not be getting the message; they will be waiting for the next punch line. Use humor in a presentation the way a chef uses spices in food—sparingly, to accent the basic flavor.

Rule Three: Avoid clumsy or self-deprecating humor. It is a bad idea to characterize yourself or your associates as louts, boobs, or just plain folks for the sake of humor, yet it is often done. Generally, no person or group should be the target of your humor.

Rule Four: Examine your delivery style. A few people simply lack the expression, the animation, the sense of timing needed to use humor effectively. If your delivery style isn't suited to it, don't use humor. Few things are as awkward, for example, as a presentation that begins with a vain attempt to get a laugh. The silence (or groans or weak tittering) makes your audience uncomfortable and puts you in a deep hole at the outset.

The Importance of Pace

While you are preparing your script, be aware of the clock. Think of the audience's ability to absorb new ideas and their implications. Are you giving them enough time? Conversely, are you dawdling—using too much time to make a relatively simple point? *Idea density* is an expression coined to describe the flow of ideas and their supporting structure. Strive to tailor the idea density— to pace the introduction of new ideas in your presentation—to your audience's ability to process the material.

Level of detail has a great deal to do with the overall pace of a presentation as well. Provide too much supporting detail and explanation and they become impatient, bored, preoccupied. Provide too little and they become lost, confused, irritated.

The Importance of Unity

In a business or technical presentation, a *frame* is the rough equivalent of the paragraph in writing. Thus, each frame should be unified, that is, designed to make a point, to make a statement and support it. Ask yourself, "What is the point of this frame?" "Have I strayed from the point by introducing unrelated information?" "Am I trying to make more than one *major point* with this frame?" (If so, use more than one frame.) And lastly, "Have I developed the idea of the frame completely?"

The following "frame" lacks unity:

> America is a nation on wheels. Beleaguered motorists everywhere are set upon by rapacious dealers and inept, careless mechanics. Truly, today's motorists creep through a jungle of predators. Confiscatory insurance costs, federal and state excise taxes, gasoline taxes, tolls, parking fees, and fines all serve to flatten the motorist's wallet. Progress in highway accident prevention has been painfully slow. Most state and local governments, realizing the plight of the motorist, provide relief with inadequate, poorly maintained roads; zealous enforcement of archaic traffic regulations; and dogged insistence that to drive is not a right, but a privilege. Today's motorists are not a minority group; they are the most abused majority on the American scene. Sunday drivers are my pet peeve.

By sticking to the development of a single idea, the following rework is much more unified:

Today's motorists are not a minority group; they are the most abused majority on the American scene. Confiscatory insurance costs, federal and state excise taxes, gasoline taxes, tolls, parking fees, and fines all serve to flatten the motorist's wallet. If this were not enough, beleaguered motorists everywhere are set upon by rapacious dealers and inept, careless mechanics. Most state and local governments, realizing the plight of the motorist, provide relief with inadequate, poorly maintained roads; zealous enforcement of archaic traffic regulations and dogged insistence that to drive is not a right, but a privilege. Truly, today's motorists creep through a jungle of predators.

The Importance of Emphasis

The frame is emphatic when it makes its point convincingly and forcefully. We tend to remember beginnings and endings. Just as with the beginning and ending of the entire presentation, concentrate on how each frame starts and concludes. It often helps to state the point at the outset and then use the frame to illustrate or support the point. If you are using induction, list and explain the facts that support the conclusion to be driven home at the end of the frame.

Transitions help to provide both emphasis and coherence. They reinforce points and help prepare an audience for the next step. A linkage at the start or end of a frame can put the whole frame in perspective. Examples of transitions:

"So much for the benefits of the new system . . . but you're probably wondering about the fixed and variable costs. Let's look at both."
"You have seen the design features of the Model 7T11. Can we produce it competitively?"
"Of all these alternatives, one promises the greatest return with the least risk: Manual Assembly. Here's why."

Use transitions to link the larger sections of your presentation. With a brief summary, let the audience know that you are concluding the discussion of a major topic; then, with an introductory link, prepare the way for the next section. On the visual side, one of the most useful devices for achieving emphasis through transitions is the *agenda slide*. Shown at the beginning of the presentation, it simply lists the subjects to be covered. For example:

AGENDA
- PURPOSE OF OUR MEETING
- CAUSES OF CAP ASSEMBLY FEED FAILURE PROBLEM
- SOLUTION 1: REDESIGN CAP FEEDER
- SOLUTION 2: REDESIGN CAP ASSEMBLY
- SOLUTION 3: MODIFY BOTH CAP AND FEEDER
- RECOMMENDATIONS
- DISCUSSION
- NEXT STEPS

During the presentation, use the same agenda slide to introduce each new agenda item. The visual should highlight the new topic in some way (underlining, bold type, color, etc.). This technique has the advantage of emphasizing:

1. What you have covered
2. What you are about to discuss next
3. What remains to be covered

This is the "you-are-here" slide.

A good script uses a variety of devices to achieve emphasis. *Repetition* is one useful method. Not dull reiteration, but careful reinforcement of one channel by the other or thoughtful restatement from various points of view. So too is *illustration or example.* Emphasis can be achieved with *analogy* (for example, comparing the flow of electricity with the flow of water) or *metaphor* ("In the cell, the ribosome is the *factory* for building amino acids").

Emphasis makes a presentation memorable.

Helpful Hints on Writing the Audio Channel of Your Script

- *Don't Put It Off*—A good script is a thoughtful construction of words and images. Writing requires care and craftsmanship and takes time. If you wait until the eleventh hour, you will pay the price of delay in the quality of your presentation.
- *Follow Your Outline*—After expending all that energy to organize your material, it's now time to reap the rewards. It would be sheer folly not to! But don't think you must follow the outline from the beginning. Start anywhere you feel comfortable, anywhere your familiarity or interest in the material will make it easier to get started. Save the difficult sections for mop-up operations later when you have completed most of the work.
- *Put Yourself in the Audience's Shoes*—Empathy is the key to effective communication. Write every word with the needs of your audience

foremost in your mind. Try to become your audience as you write the script.

• *Think Visually As You Write*—Remember that *two* channels must communicate your message. As you prepare the audio portion of your script, always consider the best way to use the visual channel in order to make your point or carry the burden of exposition. Be aware of its special power to illustrate, reinforce, make immediate, and enliven your material.

This last hint provides a timely cue to introduce the subject of visuals.

CREATING THE VISUAL CHANNEL

What's a Visual?

In broadest terms, a visual is *anything* you use to focus the eyes of your audience to gain and hold their attention. Visuals can cover the range from words, diagrams, or formulas written and drawn on a chalkboard to 35 millimeter, colored slides prepared from professionally designed and prepared artwork.

Visuals are useful for both audience and presenter. For the audience, they provide a series of road signs to highlight the content and aid in remembering the key ideas of the presentation. Visuals can contribute supporting detail, provide emphasis, and add vitality to dry material. They can be used to explain or clarify ideas at a glance, where words alone would take much more time. One classic example of this point is the diagram shown in Figure 6, used to illustrate the Pythagorean Theorem. You can say that the square of the hypotenuse is equal to the square of the two other sides of the triangle, but the words alone are not nearly as effective as actually seeing it while hearing the words.

For the presenter, the visuals act as *cue cards*. When properly designed, they provide the trigger words, phrases, and images that allow the speaker to convey all the ideas that led to the creation of the visuals in the first place. Freedom from notes, cue cards, or "cheat sheets" allows the speaker to spend most of the time doing what is most important: making contact with the audience.

Visual Media: Which One Is Best for Me?

Visual media can be divided into two classes, projected and nonprojected. Here's a list of the major examples of each:

Projected	Nonprojected
Overhead transparencies	Chalkboard (blackboard)
35mm slides	Easel pad
Lantern slides	Flip charts
Opaque projection	Models
Video projection	Handouts
Movies	The real object

One important decision you must make for every presentation you do is, "Which visual medium best suits *this* situation?" Let's look at each of the media listed above and explore the strengths and drawbacks of each.

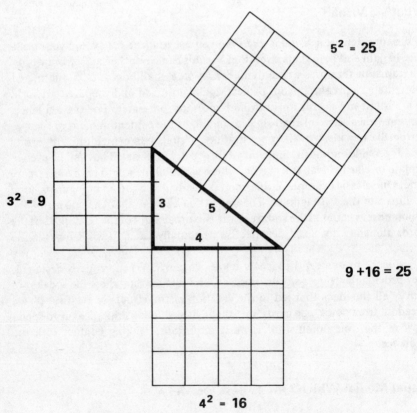

Figure 6 Explaining the Pythagorean Theorem

Projected Media

Most business and technical presentations use projected images for several reasons. Projected images:

- Are better suited to large audiences (over a dozen or so).
- Permit more control over the visual channel than most nonprojected media.
- Tend to communicate a higher degree of formality.
- Allow for more audience contact by the speaker (when used properly).

Here are the commonly used projection formats:

The Overhead Transparency

The overhead transparency (or Vu-Graph) is the most widely used medium for both business and technical presentations for many reasons:

- The projectors are easy to obtain, and the machines for making the visuals are within easy reach in most companies.
- The speaker can face the audience and use the transparency as a cue card. There is no need to look at the screen. Speakers can devote most of their time to making eye contact with the audience.
- The room does not have to be darkened. This allows interaction between the speaker and audience (and helps keep people awake!). It also makes it easier for people to take notes.
- The overhead transparency is an 8½-by-11-inch acetate sheet. The actual field size, or information area on the transparency, is about 7½ vertical inches by 9½ horizontal inches. The large field size and the design of the optical system allow you to project more information with an overhead transparency than with any other projection medium except the opaque projector. Although it is *not* a good idea to pack too much information into any visual, the overhead transparency does have a distinct edge in presentations that require complex visuals.
- The projector is at the speaker's side, which permits a measure of control over the image on the screen. The speaker can point to key features, use overlays to add information, and circle or underline important points with a grease pencil or special pens for marking transparencies. The presenter can easily switch off the projector to focus the audience's attention on the speaker and the audio channel alone. A similar effect can be achieved with 35mm and lantern slides by using an opaque or transparent slide, but the room lights must be turned up by an assistant, which is less spontaneous and a bit awkward.
- Overhead transparencies are inexpensive and easy to make.

- Because they can be made quickly, overhead transparencies make last-minute changes easy to cope with. Conventional 35mm and lantern slides, because they must be specially processed, require much longer turnaround times.
- The overall atmosphere of an overhead transparency presentation is less formal than that of 35mm. The more informal atmosphere plus the greater emphasis on the speaker, as opposed to the screen, makes overhead transparencies more effective when your goal is to encourage dialogue with your audience.
- Overhead transparencies may be reproduced on office copiers for use as handouts. Just remember it's not usually a good idea to hand out copies of your visuals *before* the presentation.

This is an impressive list of advantages, but overhead transparencies have some drawbacks. In fact, sometimes the advantages can turn into liabilities:

- Because the visuals are in front of the speaker, it is easy to use them as a crutch. Simply reading the words on the slide without adding further information not only wastes the audio channel, but it bores the audience and makes the speaker seem unprepared or even incompetent.
- The ability to control the visuals can backfire if the speaker constantly fiddles with the transparencies, points to everything in sight, or wastes time underlining or circling things unnecessarily.
- Overheads can be made to project solid blocks or lines in color, but color in overhead transparencies is expensive. Happily, the cost seems to be dropping each year.
- In order for audiences larger than 40 or so to read the visuals, the screen must be elevated and tipped forward to avoid the keystone effect, a distortion in which the top of the projected image is wider than the bottom. The problem with the keystone effect is twofold. First, the wide top and narrow bottom make an aesthetically unpleasing and amateurish appearance. Second, in a severe keystone effect, when the center of the screen is in focus, the top and the bottom of the image will be out of focus.
- The overhead projector sets a trap for unwary speakers. If they stand next to the projector, they will often be blocking the view of the screen for a few audience members. One way to avoid blocking the screen is to deliver the presentation seated. This is not as effective as delivering on your feet, where you project better, have more presence, and are in better control. (Techniques for overcoming this problem will be covered later when we discuss delivery.)

• Because of their limited use of color and continuous-tone (photographic) images, overhead transparencies are not as effective as 35mm slides for highly formal presentations, especially for audiences larger than 25 or so.

On the whole, however, with proper preparation and effective delivery techniques, the assets of overhead transparencies far outweigh the liabilities.

Two basic types of overhead projectors are available: the transmission and the reflection designs. The general appearance of each is shown in Figure 7.

The transmission type is larger and designed to be installed in a meeting or conference room. It uses a fan which can often emit heat and noise that may be annoying to those sitting very close to it. The reflection type is portable; you can carry it folded and in its case to your presentation, if that is a requirement. It usually has no fan. Light travels from the projector head down to a reflecting mirror beneath the visual. The mirror reflects the light back up to the projector head, which contains the optics for projecting the image onto the screen. This type has a few drawbacks, too. If the visual does not lie quite flat, the projector will cast a double image wherever the visual is raised above the reflector plate. The reflector plate tends to scratch easily, and the scratches show on the screen. Replacing the reflector plate is expensive.

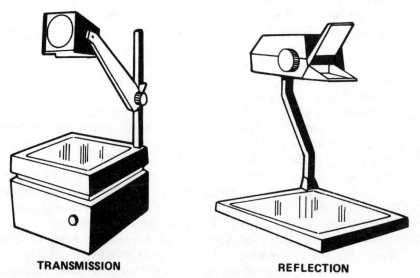

TRANSMISSION   **REFLECTION**

Figure 7   Two Types of Overhead Projector

35mm Slides

Thirty-five millimeter slides come in a close second in popularity for business presentations, and for some compelling reasons. At their best, 35mm slides are visually more stimulating than overhead transparencies. Color photography of people, places, and things lends an air of drama and realism not available with overheads or any of the nonprojected media. Color also lends interest and variety to presentations of statistical or technical material. Presentations featuring 35mm slides work best in formal presentations, especially to large audiences and when the subject is not too complex technically. This medium does have a few drawbacks, however:

- Thirty-five millimeter slides are comparatively expensive—not so much due to the cost of photography and film processing, but the major expense of manually prepared color artwork. Of course, computers are becoming ever more pervasive as tools for preparing business and technical graphics, and we will discuss computer graphics at some length in the next chapter. It is still fair to say that whether you have graphics artwork prepared for you by a professional graphics artist or you choose to spend the money for the computer hardware and software plus the output device to produce the 35mm slides (or buy the slides from a computer graphics service), 35mm slides are more expensive than overhead transparencies.
- The size of the visual field of 35mm is smaller than the overhead transparency. No more than seven or eight lines of type should be used on a single slide. Technical or business diagrams must be simple. Thus, 35mm does not lend itself easily to highly complex technical expositions. Not that such presentations are impossible to pull off; it just takes considerable effort and imagination.
- The dramatic and arresting qualities of 35mm slides tend to draw most of the audience's attention to the screen, thus reducing the speaker to a secondary role. This, of course, can be an advantage for the untrained or infrequent speaker who wants the audience to focus on the visual material while he or she enjoys the comparative comfort of being a disembodied voice from the darkness.
- In some organizations and for some audiences, 35mm slides may be frowned on as "too slick" for business or technical presentations, especially for small audiences (15 or fewer people). The importance of knowing your audience is central to dealing with this concern.
- Slides require a darkened room. The speaker must work doubly hard to make and keep contact with the audience. Avoid *completely* darkened rooms at all costs. Use a room whose lights can be controlled by a dimmer or find a way to partially block the windows. Find a compro-

mise light level that will allow your audience to take notes, see you as well as the visuals, and remain awake.

- The 35mm projector is more complex mechanically than the overhead projector. Occasionally a slide may refuse to seat itself (hang up), and on rare occasions the machine can jam. In highly formal presentations, a skilled assistant must be available to provide first aid if needed. Incidentally, the assistant will probably have to control the room lights as well.

Lantern Slides

Lantern slides are $3^{1}/_{4}$-by-4-inch, usually glass-encased transparencies. They have the same advantages as 35mm slides, but their larger field size makes them better suited to complex technical presentations. Lantern slides are often used with large audiences (over 80 to 100), especially at technical and professional symposiums. They do have some disadvantages. The projector is larger and less portable than a 35mm machine. Each slide must be manually loaded by an assistant *during* the presentation. Making the slides is a much more specialized and expensive process.

The Opaque Projector

An opaque projector projects in color anything you can get into it, such as sheets of paper and even small, flat objects. But the projector is large, heavy, bulky, hot, and noisy and requires a darkened room. It usually is permanently installed in a conference room where people use paper documents, diagrams, and tables for visuals.

Videotape and Movies

Videotapes and movies combine moving color images and sound—a potent mixture that can add realism, interest, and excitement to a presentation. Both media are "canned" forms of presentation. Although this book deals with live presentations, a quick summary of the canned variety is worthwhile, because they do have their place.

The profusion of low-cost video cameras and videocassette recorders has made video recording a frequent choice for communicating and motivating in business, government, and schools. The do-it-yourself videotapes produced by nonprofessionals tend to look that way. Professionally produced video requires hugely expensive cameras, special staging and lighting, makeup, editing, and much more. Organizations needing this level of professionalism usually rent outside facilities and expertise—normally that of a local television station. Organizations that continuously require the use of professional video facilities eventually build and staff their own. For the vast majority of the rest of us, the quality of locally produced videotapes is *good enough* for our limited communication purposes (and our limited budgets). Bear in mind, however, that for some highly formal presentations, the home-brew videotape may not suffice. People are accustomed to perfection on their home sets and may be disappointed with anything less.

Local videotape production is far less expensive and much easier to produce than are movies. On the other hand, video is not a medium originally intended for large audiences. The television screen is too small for viewing by more than a handful of people. The problem can be overcome by using several television monitors, but this is cumbersome and quite costly. Of course, if the meeting room you choose is equipped with a very large monitor (40 inches diagonal measure, for example) and your audience is roughly 15 or fewer people, the problem can be solved. Video projection systems are available for reaching larger audiences. The technology is steadily improving; image quality has become acceptable to the more fussy among us, and the prices of the systems keep dropping slowly. Video projection systems may be rented as well as purchased.

Movies are prohibitively expensive to produce and to change should it become necessary. They do have the advantage of large projection size and high image quality.

With any canned presentation, however, you must turn your audience over to the whirring, clacking machinery. If you must show your audience a videotape or movie to make a point or illustrate something especially relevant (something that requires movement and sound to show it at its best), by all means do so, but keep it brief. Introduce it carefully; explain in advance exactly what the audience should be looking for. When the canned presentation is over, bring the audience back to you with a transition that links the material they have just seen with that you will next present.

Business audiences tend to react negatively if they think they are being entertained. Be careful of canned material that does not add to the exposition or the argument sufficiently to justify using it. If the basic purpose is to rejuvenate their interest, fine; just keep it brief.

Electronic Images

Full-color electronic images created with and contained in a personal computer can be viewed on a very large video monitor or through video projection. Another device is available that acts as an "electronic overhead transparency." The small, portable, liquid crystal display (LCD) device fits on a transmission type overhead projector and receives electronic imaging information from the personal computer. Black-and-white (monochrome) or color

Figure 8 LCD Projection System (Courtesy Telex Communications, Inc.)

computer images are projected directly onto the screen. Figure 8 shows the components of a typical LCD projection system.

Computer-driven presentations are becoming increasingly common. Producing the visuals is quick and inexpensive, and making even last-minute changes is easy. The overall effect is suitable for a wide range of presentations, from informal to highly formal.

On the downside, the equipment and the software are not in everyone's budget, although prices are continually dropping. Considerable training is necessary to use the software, the computer, and the viewing equipment effectively. Computer-driven presentations work best with small audiences. Yes, video projection systems are improving, but there's still room for advancement in the quality of very large projected images.

Nonprojected Media

Chalkboard

Chalkboard (or whiteboard) is the least satisfying of the nonprojected media because the presenter must *create* the visual during the presentation. Writing on the board requires turning away from your audience for long periods. Each break in eye contact is a withdrawal. Good presenters know they must maintain contact by speaking as they write or draw on the chalkboard, but it is still less than ideal. Some speakers become skilled at writing on the board while still looking at the audience. Another problem is blocking the audience's view of the chalkboard while you write. Creating the visual takes time—time that can be better spent in other ways. On the plus side, the chalkboard is inexpensive (providing you have one available) and flexible in that you can write, add detail, change, and erase at will. The chalkboard is particularly effective when the speaker wants to involve the audience and capture their ideas and comments.

Easel Pad

An easel pad is a large (usually 19-by-24-inch) pad of paper mounted on an easel. Its advantage is that the visual (or artwork) can be prepared in advance. The presenter simply turns the page to show the next visual. If the speaker uses the blank pad to draw or write on during the presentation, the advantage is lost. The easel pad then becomes a "paper chalkboard." The easel pad has other advantages: It is inexpensive, flexible, and easy to use. The disadvantages include its small size, which rules it out for audiences larger than about 15 people. Also, the easel pad has an informal quality that can make it ill-suited to highly formal presentations. Like the chalkboard, the easel pad can be used to capture ideas, questions, and comments from your audience.

Flip Charts

Flip charts are stiff, white cardboard sheets (usually Bainbridge Board) on which artwork is printed or drawn. A product called foam board attaches the thin, white board to a thicker plastic base for rigidity. They can be cut to any size, although the most common size is 20 by 40 inches. Flip charts may be used with a variety of easels.

One advantage of flipcharts is their usefulness in informal presentations where projection equipment is unavailable, unworkable, or undesirable. Flip charts work best with small audiences (15 or fewer people). Occasionally you may need to show an accumulation of visuals to an audience, leaving each one in view as you progress. Flip charts work well in such a case; so does the easel pad if you tear the sheets from the pad, then tape them to the wall.

Flip charts also have several disadvantages. In fact, they are seldom desirable for presentations for several reasons. First, the expensive (usually done manually by an artist or illustrator) artwork is applied directly to the chart, then that original artwork goes into combat to be scuffed, smudged, scarred, dog-eared, even lost. It is preferable to reproduce the original artwork on a transparency or 35mm slide. One can always replace a slide as long as the original artwork is kept intact. Second, flip charts, especially the large ones, are cumbersome to transport and often awkward to use. Third, they do not work well with large audiences. An overhead transparency, for example, can project the same amount of information as a flip chart, but on a large screen. Fourth, they do not lend themselves to easy reproduction in reduced format. Finally, it normally is far easier to change the artwork for transparencies than it is to "change" a flip chart. Usually the entire chart must be redone.

Models and Mockups

Models are useful for replicating a large object on a smaller scale, such as buildings, machines, floor plans, and roadways. The presentation can use the actual model and/or photographs of it for large audiences. Models are usually limited to presentations in which the stakes are high enough to justify the considerable expense of building them.

A mockup is a *full-size* model, built from cardboard, plywood, or other materials less expensive than the original. Mockups are usually prepared for study purposes but can be occasionally used for presentations as well.

Handouts

Technically, handouts are anything you put in the hands of your audience, such as an object or a sheet of paper containing information. Some refer to them as "pass-outs." Unfortunately, both terms have negative overtones.

Handouts can be used as visuals during a presentation. They can provide an outline that the audience can fill in with its own notes. They do have drawbacks. First it takes time to distribute the handout. You will need to find ways to hold the audience's attention and introduce the handout during distribution. (Ask for volunteers to pass out material while you spend your time preparing your audience for it.) Second, the mere presence of a handout is a distraction. Audience members will want to examine it and extract information at their own pace, which means that your words will not reach most of them. The best way to deal with this problem is to give the audience some time to get familiar with the handout before you begin to discuss it. Allow a little intellectual play before beginning the work of exposition. Then you must carefully guide your audience through the handout as if it were any other type of visual.

The second and most common use of handouts is to give the audience a record of the presentation for later reference. This second application should not be confused with using the handout as a visual. If you wish to provide reference material, distribute it *after* the presentation is over, when it will not distract your audience.

Never begin a presentation by distributing handouts. You will lose your audience at the most critical time: at the beginning, when you most need them.

The Real Object

Depending on the circumstances, you can use anything in the environment as a visual, including field trips, plant tours, and equipment demonstrations. Several problems must be considered, however:

1. Getting your audience to and from the site
2. Narrowing their attention to the specific details you wish to present

3. The presence of distractions in the environment, such as high noise levels
4. Physical limitations of the environment; for example, the space that the audience must occupy may be so small that only a veteran submarine captain can concentrate. The larger the audience, the more likely some members will not be able to *see* what you wish to show them.

The real object can be effective as a visual, sometimes dramatically so, but be sensitive to possible logistical and physical problems.

Which Visual Medium?

As a summary, Table 3 lists the visual formats discussed here and compares them by the most important criteria.

Choosing Effective Visuals

Once you have chosen the medium to convey the visual part of your message, you must continue to make choices. As you prepare your script, you must select from all those available the one type of visual that best communicates the point of each frame. You must keep asking, "What is the best way to explain, support, illustrate, emphasize, reinforce, or prove this idea or point?"

The types of images you may choose include diagrams, tables, charts, graphs, words, schematics, illustrations, cartoons, maps, photographs, or "live" objects. Later, we will look at most of these types of visuals in detail. But for the purposes of planning your script, what are the the qualities that make *any* visual effective?

General Rules for Effective Visuals

Unity means that each visual should make a single point. Use a title or focus headline to capture that point. With the speaker's help, the visual should make the point completely in no more than two to three minutes. Unity also means that all the elements in the visual act together to focus on that single point.

Simplicity is the key to visuals that work. The purpose of a visual is to make ideas and relationships simple and memorable. Every line, word, number—every graphic element—should have a function. Nothing of note should appear on the screen that does not get mentioned by the speaker.

Avoid visuals that are fancy purely for the sake of being creative or visually impressive. This only dilutes the impact of the visual. Color, too, should be functional and not merely decorative.

Economy means not adding one unnecessary word or number. The impact of the visual should stand out immediately and not be hidden in a thicket

Table 3 Selecting a Visual Medium

Medium	Cost	Portability	For Complex Visuals	Degree of Formality	Rough Size of Audience	Lead Time	Comments
Chalkboard	0	0	Fair	Low	Small to medium	0	Slow, cumbersome, poor audience contact
Easel Pad	Low	Poor	Poor	Low	Small	Short	Good for small, informal, non-complex presentations
Flip Charts	Medium to high	Poor to fair	Fair	Fair	Small	Medium to long	Often cumbersome, expensive
Models	Very high	Depends on size	Very good	Excellent	Small	Very long	Cost must be justified, can be highly effective
The Real Object	Depends	Depends on size	Very good	Good	Small to medium	0	Be aware of logistics and the environment
Overhead Transparencies	Medium	Depends on type	Very good	Good	Medium to large	Short	Popular, quick, may become a "crutch"
35mm Slides	Medium to high	Very good	Fair	Excellent	Medium to very large	Medium	Color, flexibility, live photographs, small field size
Lantern Slides	Medium to high	Poor	Good	Excellent	Medium to very large	Medium to long	Good for large groups and complex data
Opaque Projection	Low	Very poor	Very good	Low to fair	Small to medium	Short	Heavy, bulky, noisy, etc. Okay for informal meetings
Videotape	Medium to high	Very poor	Poor to fair	Good to very good	Small	Short to medium	Limited to small groups, flexible, captures sound and movement
Movies	Extremely high	Fair	Very good	Excellent	Medium to very large	Very long	Potent visual tool, but with many drawbacks
Electronic Images	High at first	0	Good	Excellent	Small to medium	Short	After initial costs/training, very cost effective, flexible

of details and supporting information. Remember, *the speaker provides the supporting details, not the visual.* One of the most powerful elements of a good visual is blank space—space that frames the content and guides the audience's attention to the message.

Legibility means that everyone in the room is able to recognize the smallest symbol, letter, or line in the visual. The usual tendency is to cram too much text, too many numbers, too many curves, too many bars or too many "pieces of pie" in visuals.

How can you know if the visual will be legible when projected? Use the *rule of eight.* View the artwork at a distance of eight times the height of the image. Measure the top-to-bottom distance of the image (let's say it is six inches). View the artwork at a distance eight times the image height (48 inches). If you can read the text and the lines are distinct, the visual will be legible *up to eight times the distance of the projected image.* Let's assume you will be projecting the image on a six-foot-high screen. The image will be legible up to 48 feet away. Use good contrast between the background and foreground. For 35mm slides, use dark-colored backgrounds, lighter (or white) foregrounds. For overhead transparencies, use light colored or transparent backgrounds and dark colored or black letters. Avoid black backgrounds in any type of visual. Indeed, a black background with clear letters can produce unpleasant optical effects. Avoid black letters on dark colored backgrounds (blue, purple, dark green).

One of the most common violations of the legibility rule is *using documents for visuals.* Documents are meant to be read by individuals at their own pace and at a distance of 12 to 14 inches. They can contain up to 500 words per page. *Documents and working papers or diagrams of any type are totally unsuitable for visuals.* Visuals are meant to focus audience attention on the main points of the presentation and to complement the words of the speaker. Documents and visuals have radically different functions. Overhead transparencies that are copies of documents are unreadable when projected onto a screen.

The next time you are in the audience of a presentation whose first visual is a *memo,* ask the speaker if you are expected to read the whole thing or just part of it . . . and if just a part, which part . . . and could he refrain from talking to give you time to read it? Two things will likely happen: That speaker will never use a memo as a visual again, and you will never be invited to attend another of that person's presentations (be thankful).

Consistency requires that the same type style and art style be used for all the visuals. Scales should be consistent as well. Mixing a variety of different styles not only looks amateurish, it gives the audience the impression that you have cobbled up a collection of visuals from past presentations.

Clarity is important. The audience should be able to grasp the main idea of the visual in 10 to 15 seconds. Do not give your audience ugly riddles to solve. A visual aid is just that—an *aid* to understanding, not a source of confusion. *Color* can help clarity. Use colors to show different paths or systems in a diagram, or to identify different parts in an assembly, or curves in a graph. Always give each visual a prominent *title* that captures the essence of the visual's message. *Label* every important part of the visual, but only the parts that are necessary to understanding. Do whatever you can to help the audience get the point quickly and without a lot of head scratching.

You may have an urge to show your audience a hopelessly complicated visual, one which will take 30 minutes of study to begin to decipher. You don't expect your audience will understand it; you just want to give them a sense of how terribly complicated your subject is! *Please stifle that urge.*

Appropriateness. Visuals should be appropriate to the subject, the audience, and the situation. Be especially careful of cartoons and other humorous visuals. As with the audio channel, avoid humor that exploits, that is self-deprecating, that is tactless, or that may offend.

Quality. Remember, the quality of your visuals conveys a message. If they are scratched or contain sloppy lettering or clumsy artwork, the visuals convey an impression much like that of showing up at a fancy affair with a tuxedo and tennis shoes.

Quality often reflects the degree of formality of a presentation—the more formal, the better the quality. The budget, resources, and time available also influence quality. Whatever the situation and the restraints, the quality of your visuals should be the best you can manage.

Time—not money—is too often the factor that limits quality. It takes time to prepare artwork, just as it takes time to produce high-quality audiovisual materials. Plan your schedule to allow enough time for quality. All the money in the world and all the political clout available cannot buy back time.

THE IMPORTANCE OF BALANCE

The most common flaw in script preparation for a presentation is a lack of balance between the audio and the visual channels. The special power of the audiovisual presentation derives in part from its two-channel approach to communication. It is vital that both channels contribute equally to the work. Here is a list of common problems that can cause the channels to get out of balance.

Overloading

This occurs when the visual is so complex or so packed with information that the audience cannot cope with both channels simultaneously. When you use such a visual, you, in effect, are saying to your audience, *"You must choose between listening to me or absorbing what you are seeing."* The audience will nearly always choose the visual channel because it is more arresting, because they can process visual information at their own pace, and because they can process information much faster with their eyes than with their ears. Your voice, to which they have become accustomed, will fade into the background. Your audience will be hearing you but not listening to you.

How do you prevent overloading the channels? First, avoid cramming too much information into one visual. Break the material into several manageable slides or transparencies. Next, if a complex visual must be used, show it in stages by progressively adding more material and discussing the new material at each stage. In that way you can gradually guide your audience through the complexities of your material. Lastly, if you *must* show a visual that will cause overloading, stop talking. Give your audience enough time to process the information. In such a case, the audio portion of the script might go as follows: "This table shows the managerial, professional, clerical, and production staffing needs we will encounter in the next 24 months." (Pause.) When you use the visual, wait until the last person has finished reading the material before continuing. True, it's awkward, but the alternative—to keep talking to an audience whose interests are elsewhere—is unacceptable.

Weak Visual Channel

Have you ever listened to a person speak for five minutes while displaying a one-word visual? Next time it happens, watch the audience. Those who are paying attention will either be looking at the speaker or restlessly glancing at both the speaker and the screen. Those who have left the room mentally will be gazing at that single word as if it had hypnotic power.

We seldom see one-word visuals, but a similar practice, that of using the visual channel for merely showing *topics*, is all too common. Usually the speaker fills in the supporting detail by dull readings from notes. If the *subtopics* were included in the visual, however, the speaker would not need notes or cue cards, and the audience would have a more interesting, useful, "meaty" visual channel.

Failure to Integrate the Two Channels

Each channel should provide information. If the speaker is simply reading the visuals to the audience, the audio channel adds nothing. In fact, the speaker is unnecessary. The audience can read without anyone's help. Balance in a script means that the channels complement each other. Each channel should do some of the work. Balance also means that the content of the sounds and the images is closely related, working in harmony to accomplish the mission of each frame. In short, don't show one thing and talk about something else, and don't show something and not talk about it.

THE MOST OVERLOOKED REASON FOR PREPARING A SCRIPT

Before we leave the subject of script preparation, we need to explore the deeper purpose of having any script at all.

The reason for preparing a script is not just to assure that the audience will be receiving a balanced flow of audio and visual information, although that's an important goal.

And the reason for preparing the script is *not* to select exactly the right words to say (or worse, to read) to your audience. The words are not all that important; it's the *ideas* that matter most. If you give the presentation several times and you use different words each time to convey the same ideas, that's fine. Exact wording is critical in diplomatic speeches or presentations involving precise legal language, but not in most business or technical presentations. This is not a license to use words imprecisely, simply a reminder that 99 percent of the time, the way you express your ideas is perfectly acceptable, and memorizing or reading words is not necessary—in fact, it is disruptive. It's too easy to forget the exact wording, and when you do forget, you are likely to stumble or freeze.

No, the most important reason for preparing a script is the creation of visual "triggers" for the memory.

Visual triggers (or mnemonics) allow you to speak to all of the ideas in your presentation without referring to notes or cue cards. Here's how it works as you prepare your script: Following your outline, you write all the words necessary to convey your ideas in the frame of the presentation. Now you turn your attention to the visual channel. If the visual is a text slide, you *extract only the key words, the headlines, the triggers that will allow you to address all the ideas in the frame in your own words.* The visual is a road map for the audience, but it is a *cue card* for you. Similarly, if the frame uses a diagram or chart or other graphic for a visual, you simply address the main points that the visual conveys—the points that made you choose that form of visual in the first place.

Each frame lasts from one to three minutes or so; think of each frame as a little speech. We all have millions of little speeches in us. They just need to be triggered. For example:

- What's your pet peeve?
- Describe the worst illness you have experienced.
- Tell your favorite joke.
- Describe the greatest gift you have ever received.
- What teacher do you remember vividly?
- Describe your most embarrassing moment.

The tapes to those little speeches are inside our heads, waiting to be triggered. When you prepare a script you assemble a whole collection of such tapes. Some existed already; some are new. The script allows you to plan the *visual* triggers that will start those mental tapes playing when you need them.

Those visual triggers are one of the most important reasons for preparing a script.

CHOICES

Preparing a script is an exercise in making choices. You must choose the most suitable *words* to convey your message in the audio channel. You must choose the *visual medium* (or combination of media) that will best satisfy the requirements of your presentation. Then you must choose, frame by frame, the *type of visual* that best supports, illustrates, amplifies, reinforces, or proves the information in the audio channel. Choose wisely and well!

After all those choices are made, your script serves as a blueprint for the design and production of the visuals. That design and production and its new choices now await us.

8

Produce Your Visuals

The script that you prepared is a program for the ideas your audience will hear and the images they will view to support, amplify, highlight, and punctuate those ideas. The script describes those images and when necessary explains their intent. Now it is time to convert those descriptions to real images. As you will see, the range of choices for both the design and production of visuals is huge.

VISUALS ON A SHOESTRING

What resources are available to you? Situations vary widely. Let's begin our inquiry at the lower end of the spectrum, with those who choose (or are forced) to create their own artwork and produce their own visuals. This requires a collection of skills not commonly found in one person—graphic design and artistic ability plus skills in reproducing the artwork in photographic or thermographic form. Visuals produced by individuals (and the team of boss and assistant) are often something less than ideal. Such presentations are typically prepared using a typewriter to create text and tables. Usually the visuals are overhead transparencies created on the local office copier or other nearby electrostatic processor. Presentations using these visuals are often nothing more than projected, visual reports in which the audience's role is to read page after page of verbatim text and endless columns of numbers. Incidentally, credit for these novacaine-for-the-mind presentations goes to the boss, not the obedient but misguided assistant.

Using a typewriter for making effective overhead transparencies is never easy, but it can be done. Begin by making sure the typewriter's font, or letters, are clean. *Always* use a carbon—not a fabric—ribbon. The type style should be large, bold and uncluttered. Choose a type style that will be easy to read. Many people prefer Univers or a typeface resembling it (Helvetica is another example.).

Univers is a sans serif typeface; it has no extensions at the ends of its letters. Many prefer the clean lines of a sans serif type, especially for headings. However, some specialists in typography urge that a type *with* serifs is more readable, because the serifs help to create the illusion of lines at the top and bottom of the letters. These suggested "lines" help to guide the reader's eye.

This Is A Sample Of Times Roman Bold, A Typeface With Serifs.

Avoid script type faces; they quickly become tiring to read.

The most important thing to remember is that if the type isn't big enough to read, no typeface will work.

Avoid vertical lettering:

i
t
,
s

h
a
r
d

t
o

r
e
a
d

The choice of paper is critical. *Avoid standard bond paper;* its surface is too rough for sharp, dense, unbroken letters. Use a 20-pound sulfite paper, which has no rag content. Office copy machine paper (used in plain-paper office copiers) is satisfactory, but not as good. Be sure the typewriter's impression control is set to give the best results. Lastly, the paper should be inserted in the typewriter *sideways*. Remember, the image field size of the overhead transparency is only 7 1/2 inches high, but 9 1/2 inches wide. One must overcome the normal tendency to insert the paper in the typewriter as if one were going to type a letter. Overhead transparencies are wider than they are high.

COMPUTER-GENERATED PRESENTATION GRAPHICS

The scenes of people using typewriters are beginning to fade into history. The personal computer is changing the way individuals can create and produce their own visuals, and the changes are dramatic.

The terms *desktop publishing* and *desktop presentations* were coined to describe these changes in the ways we produce published materials and presentation visuals. The breakthrough resulted from the merging of several technologies:

- Small, relatively powerful, easy-to-use, modestly priced personal computers
- Computer programs that allow us to create a great variety of graphic images and combine text with those images
- Inexpensive scanning devices that enable us to "read" existing images into the computer and then modify them to suit our needs
- The revolution in non-impact printing—low-cost ink jet printers and laser printers that produce images and near-typeset-quality text directly onto transparency material
- The availability of low-cost video printers—devices that produce 35mm color slides directly from computer-generated images

These tools have made it possible for individuals to produce visuals of near professional quality. For example, one of the most compelling advantages of desktop presentations is the ability to use a wide range of typefaces and type styles. Figure 9 shows the appearance of a text visual prepared with both a typewriter and a computer-driven laser printer.

Another feature of desktop presentations is that decisions of style can be made by the graphics software programs. Charts and graphs can be selected from a catalog, for example. Once you have chosen the type of chart you wish to use, the software can select the scale, choose the position, size, and type style of the heading and all supporting text, and then execute the graphic elements in a highly readable fashion. The preparer need only fill in the numerical data and text.

Will the result be as professional-looking as work done by a graphic artist or illustrator? Emphatically not. But the decisions made by the computer are more than satisfactory for all but the most formal of presentations.

ADVANTAGES of
TYPESET vs TYPEWRITTEN VISUALS

- Improved Reading Speed

- Professional Appearance

- Higher Credibility

- More Appealing

- More Persuasive

- More Memorable

- Greater Overall Impact

ADVANTAGES of
TYPESET vs TYPEWRITTEN VISUALS

- **Improved Reading Speed**

- **Professional Appearance**

- **Higher Credibility**

- **More Appealing**

- **More Persuasive**

- **More Memorable**

- **Greater Overall Impact**

Figure 9 Typewriter (top of page) vs. Laser Printer (bottom)

Another powerful advantage of computer-generated images, of course, is the ability to make last-minute changes easily. Changing manually produced artwork is usually much more time-consuming and difficult. Moreover, last-minute changes often tend to *look* last-minute when they are done manually.

The cost of desktop-presentation hardware is constantly edging down-ward. These technologies are within reach of nearly every organization's purse. Perhaps the larger costs are the time needed to learn how to use the computer and the software plus the inefficiencies that cannot be avoided while one is learning. Computerphobia may also be an obstacle in some organizations. Once these hurdles are cleared and the system functions normally, overhead transparencies can be *produced* for pennies. *Designing* the visual often takes about the same amount of time as conventional methods. The great time saver is the ability to make changes with little effort.

Perhaps you already have access to a personal computer for your business or technical work. Perhaps you are also aware of the range of software tools available to help you with the task of writing: programs to help organize your material (outline generators or "idea processors"), spelling checkers that tell you—sometimes as you are typing it—that you have misspelled a word and substitute the correctly spelled version of the word at your command, programs that check for mistakes in grammar and for poor writing, and electronic thesauruses that will display every synonym and antonym of the word you used and wish to improve *(better, correct, rectify, mend, gain, remedy, set right)*.

Perhaps, however, you are not aware of the wide range of software packages that are available to help you with preparing and even displaying business and technical presentation graphics. Here are some examples:

- *Chart Programs* allow you to create charts from your data. They feature a surprisingly complete array of charts and diagrams. The best of these programs will also let you create visuals that contain only words.
- *Paint Programs* allow you to create your own freehand pictures. You become the artist in complete control of creating the graphic. These programs use a technique called bit mapping, which allows you to control every pixel, or picture element, on the screen. The visual results can be truly impressive.
- *Draw Programs* are used to make line drawings. These programs allow you to construct graphic images from basic geometric shapes, such as lines, circles, boxes. Draw programs are used to create organization charts, flow charts, and diagrams. Draw programs are a bit harder to learn than paint programs, but they allow greater flexibility in editing and much higher quality output on laser printers. Hybrid programs are also available that combine both draw and paint techniques. Figure 10 shows examples of typical chart, paint, and draw computer programs.
- *Enhancement Programs* let you improve an existing computer generated graphic. For example, a graphic from Lotus 1-2-3, a popular spreadsheet, data base, and business graphics program, may be fine for analysis, but unacceptably crude for presentation. An enhance-

1988 USE STATISTICS

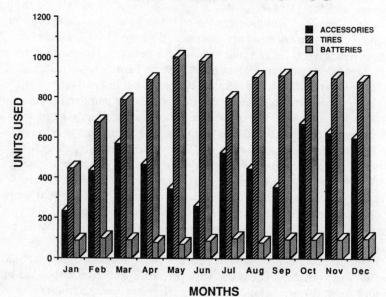

Figure 10A   Chart Program

Figure 10B   Paint Program

DESKTOP PUBLISHING

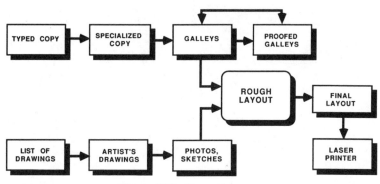

Figure 10C   Draw Program

ment program will allow you to improve the resolution and the color, plus add your own "clip art."

- *Presentation Set Up Programs* accept graphic images from other programs and allow you to arrange them in sequence for presentation, either by a very large (40″) monitor or video projection. The visuals can be programmed to run automatically or on your command. The visuals can be programmed to change with a variety of special effects (dissolves, wipes, overlays, etc.).

- *Special Technical Graphics Programs* range from mapping programs to mathematical notation, chemical symbol representation, engineering design (CAD), statistical charting and technical illustration.

A word about computer hardware. Graphics programs may require a device called a *graphics card* to provide high image resolution and control all the pixels in the display screen. Most graphics programs also require an input device other than a keyboard. The device called a *mouse* has become the de facto standard, although pressure sensitive *digitizing tablets* are also popular because they provide the natural feeling of drawing (see Figure 11).

A device called an *input scanner* converts images on paper to digital information, which can be changed once it is in the computer. Low resolution (300 to 400 dots per inch) black-and-white scanners are relatively inexpensive.

The Macintosh Computer, introduced by Apple Computer, has its own graphics capability and comes with a mouse pointing device. A standard IBM PC requires the addition of a graphics card, a high resolution monitor, and a mouse to make use of the graphics programs described earlier. Current IBM models do have graphics capability without additional hardware.

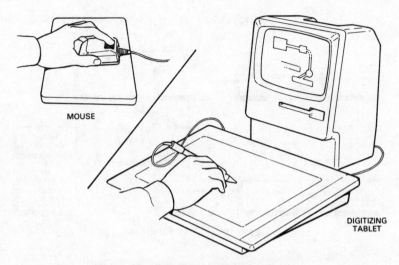

MOUSE

DIGITIZING
TABLET

Figure 11   Pointing and Drawing Devices

Don't forget an output device. You will need either a color ink jet printer, a color pen plotter, a laser printer (preferably color), and/or a 35mm color film recorder such as the Polaroid Palette to produce high-quality hard copy or slides. A black-and-white dot matrix printer will not yield acceptable graphics for any but the most informal of presentations.

Are there any reasons for *not* acquiring your own visual producing equipment? As you may have suspected, yes, there are several. First, if you make presentations infrequently, the costs in money and training are not justified. Second, once you purchase equipment, it becomes vulnerable to obsolescence, and advances in this field are occurring with dazzling speed. Third, owning your own equipment requires that you become responsible for maintenance, repairs, expensive service contracts, and problems with exasperating breakdowns. Fourth, the inexpensive, personal computer–based graphics and visual equipment does not provide the high *resolution* one is accustomed to with professionally produced visuals. Inexpensive laser printers, for example, produce images at 300 to 400 dots per inch (DPI). Truly high resolution images, however, require 2000 to 2400 DPI. Resolution this high requires an output device costing $50,000 or more. Lastly, the colors produced in expensive, professional film recorders is clearer, more vibrant, and more consistent.

Another option is to create your own visuals using the computer, then send those digitally encoded images over telephone wires (with a device called a modem) to a service bureau, which will produce the images on the most sophisticated (and expensive) film recorders available, and return them to you as 35mm slides in about a day. This option provides control over the design of the visual, highest quality output, and low initial cost. But be careful—the lengthy turnaround time means that you probably can't tolerate *any* last-minute changes.

USING PROFESSIONAL AUDIOVISUAL SERVICES

If you do not have the equipment, the ability, the time, or the desire to prepare your own visuals, it is likely that your company or organization has a group, section, or department that provides professional help with visual design and production. This group is likely to have a fully equipped, high-quality presentation production facility with computer equipment and output devices (laser typesetters and film recorders) that will provide you with professional-quality visuals. The in-house service group also has the advantage of providing you with tighter security should your presentation deal with confidential technical or strategic business information.

If producing your own visuals on a typewriter and photocopier is at one end of the spectrum, at the opposite end is to contract the entire process—conception, design, creation, production—to an outside audiovisual firm. The results are almost always exceptional—but so is the cost. Specialty graphics production houses tend to be used for presentations of great importance, such as annual sales meetings or shareholders' meetings. As always, the decision is made after weighing the cost of the service against the size of one's budget and the importance of achieving the objectives of the presentation.

Using Audiovisual Services Effectively

Should you decide to use the audiovisual services of either your own organization or an outside firm, be aware that careful thought and planning can save hundreds—even thousands—of dollars:

- Ask for an estimate of the cost of designing and producing your visuals. If the cost is too high for your budget, ask for less costly alternatives.
- Ask to see samples of the types of visuals you will be receiving. Be certain they represent what you need.
- Allow as much time as possible for the service to produce the visuals. Last-minute, rush requests always incur large extra costs, especially from outside service bureaus.
- Be absolutely certain that the graphics information or design requirements and the text are in final form. *Never use an audiovisual service as a means of generating drafts.* Changes to "final" visuals are the biggest reason for cost overruns.

- Provide clear, unambiguous instructions and input information. Artists and typesetters who must puzzle over cryptic or undecipherable materials waste time and often produce unwanted results, which must be redone.
- Ask to proof all final artwork before it goes on for production into visuals. It is less expensive to correct at this stage than after the visual has been made.
- Extremely complex graphics are also extremely expensive. Ask for help in simplifying or even eliminating manual artwork where possible.
- Be aware of your audience, the physical setting, the degree of formality, and what you are trying to accomplish with your visuals.

TYPES OF VISUALS

So much for the options available for producing the visuals. Let's now turn to the types of visuals available and discuss when and how to use each type.

Text Slides

The most common problem with text—or word—slides is simply using too many words. *Never use complete sentences.* The visual should show the smallest number of key words—or "headlines"—that will capture the ideas you wish to convey.

The two slides shown in Figure 12 illustrate this point. Both slides will be read by the audience, but the first (A) is like a report. The speaker cannot add anything to the written message. With slide A, the speaker is forced to choose between two unsatisfactory courses: either repeating the written words to the audience, or pausing in silence to give them time to read it. Both options are awkward and boring. With slide B, the audio channel comes alive; the speaker completes the story by providing supporting detail, examples, emphasis.

Slide B serves *two* functions: It highlights the main thrust of the speaker's points for the audience, and it becomes a *cue card* for the speaker.

Use the *rule of sevens* for text slides. Limit the number of lines and the number of words per line to seven. If you can't make your point with 49 words, you probably should rethink it.

Use bullets (•) or dashes to emphasize key points. If the artwork for the visual is being typed, the 8 1/2-by-11-inch sheets of paper should be inserted horizontally. The projection format for both 35mm and overhead transparencies is wider than it is tall.

**AREAS OF CONCERN WITH THE
Q.C./LINE INTERFACE**

The lack of sufficient staff in Q.C. is causing
delays in releasing product.

The entire time must be spent responding to
problems with production, not helping find
ways to improve quality.

Many line people don't understand the necessity
for charging the costs of Quality Control to the
product, nor do they understand the basis for the
charges.

Frictions and misunderstandings seem to characterize the dealings of Q.C. and line people.

Too Wordy

PROBLEMS:

- **LACK OF PEOPLE = DELAYS**
- **REACTION VS. PROACTION**
- **CHARGEBACK**
- **COMMUNICATION**

Figure 12 Key Words Only

Even at their best, text slides are not visually stimulating. Unfortunately, this most abstract form of visual tends to be overused. When planning your visuals, ask yourself if a picture or the combination of pictures and text can be used to make your points more vividly than text alone.

Tables

Probably the most abused form of visual, tables are also the most commonly used in business presentations. Tables compare statistical information, usually columns of figures, and most often each column represents a point in time. Strictly speaking, a table is any tabular arrangement of information, so columns of text would also be considered a "table."

A presentation consisting of an unbroken series of tables is difficult enough for an audience, but if the tables themselves are difficult to interpret, the result is disastrous. Here are some suggestions for making tables easy to read and understand:

- Be ruthless with numbers; use the fewest possible that will still convey the point of the visual. Try not to exceed 20 numbers.
- Combine numbers into larger sums wherever possible; eliminate any number that does not contribute significantly to the visual.
- Do not use one huge table when you can split the data into two or three smaller tables. Remember—use no more than five or six columns per visual.
- Have a title that states the point of the visual. Put it at the top. Include a date below the table.
- Label the columns clearly at the top of each column. Show the units (dollars or tons, for example). On the left, label the statistics being compared.
- Avoid footnotes. Tables are difficult enough without creating yet another obstacle for the audience to contend with.
- Use thin lines sparingly if you need them to improve readability.
- Be consistent. Do not mix pounds and tons, years and months, gross and net.
- Align decimal points vertically.
- Highlight the most important numbers with boxes, underlining, or color.
- If arithmetic operations are not obvious, state them: "(less)" or "Less Depreciation Expense."
- Eliminate zeros by expressing numbers in thousands or millions, if possible.
- Show negative numbers in parentheses, not with minus signs.

- Lastly, before deciding to use a table, ask if the same information can be shown using graphics. Charts, graphs, diagrams, and statistical maps are all preferable to tables. Knowing your audience is crucial in this regard. Some executives are distinctly uncomfortable with graphics and view such "shortcuts" with suspicion.

For an illustration of these points, study Table 4. Try to remember all the things that puzzle you—all the unanswered questions posed by the table. Indeed, if this table were used as a visual, it would take the audience 10 to 15 minutes to decipher it. Even then the table would not have yielded up all its secrets. (What, for example, is meant by "Sales"?)

Now examine Table 5, which deals with with the same subject, but presents it more clearly and more suitably for a visual.

Now look at both tables. Compare the titles, the headings, the level of detail, and finally, the differences in typography. Table 4 was created with a standard typewriter. Table 5 was created on typesetting equipment. Even though Table 5 may not be the ideal way to present the information, it is an enormous improvement over the original version.

Statistical Graphics

As mentioned earlier, graphics can be much more effective as visuals than words and numbers alone. The latter are rooted in the tradition of writing. Reports, memos, and the like must stand on their own; they must be self-contained. Presentations, in contrast, are conducted live, with participants in each other's presence and with a speaker's voice to help explain and interpret the visual information being shown.

Tables are useful if the aim is to look at the actual numbers. Graphics, on the other hand, are useful for showing *trends, directions, comparisons, and interrelationships*. Part of the special power of graphics is the ability to show information *at a glance*. Graphics of any kind make it possible to visualize numerical information. Tables and text appeal to the left brain, which specializes in verbal (and other symbolic) processing, logic, and step-by-step reasoning. Graphics appeal to the right brain, which specializes in pattern recognition, intuition, insight, and forming mental pictures.

Let's examine the most commonly used types of statistical graphics.

Bar Graphs

Figure 13 shows 12 of the the most often used types of bar graphs. The *column chart* (A), or vertical bar chart, is most useful for showing a variable over a series of points in time—for example, annual sales or monthly expenses. The graphic impact is best when you wish to contrast the differences or highlight the magnitude of changes from one period to another.

Table 4 First Draft Prepared with a Typewriter

COST ESTIMATE

New Plastics Plant

End of	1/2 year 170,000 lb 73¢ lb	1 year 454,000 lb 73¢ lb	1-1/2 years 1,000,000 lb/yr 73¢ lb	2 years 1,500,000 lb/yr 73¢ lb	2-1/2 years 2,000,000 lb/yr 70¢ lb	3 years 3,000,000 lb/yr 68¢ lb
Annual Sales Rate	$123,000	$358,000	$730,000	$1,095,000	$1,400,000	$2,040,000
Material	77,000(45¢ lb)	182,000(40¢ lb)	400,000	600,000	800,000	1,200,000
Labor	27,000	47,000	100,000	150,000	200,000	300,000
GROSS PROFIT	19,000	129,000	230,000	345,000	400,000	540,000
Factory Overhead	82,500	82,500	82,500	82,500	100,000	100,000
R & D	12,000	12,000	20,000	30,000	35,000	40,000
Administration	51,000	51,000	51,000	51,000	55,000	60,000
Sales	30,500	30,500	35,500	40,000	40,000	50,000
Total	280,000	405,000	689,000	953,500	1,230,000	1,750,000
Net Cash Flow	-157,000	- 47,000	41,000	141,500	170,000	290,000
Depreciation	33,000	36,000	40,000	50,000	60,000	75,000
Total Loss	-$190,000	-$ 83,000	+$ 1,000	+$ 91,500	+$ 110,000	+$ 215,000

Table 5   Final Typeset Draft

3-YEAR PROFIT PROJECTION: NEW PLASTICS PLANT

	YEAR 1	YEAR 2	YEAR 3
UNIT STATISTICS			
ANNUAL PRODUCTION RATE(000)	454	1500	3000
PRICE PER POUND ($)	.73	.73	.68
PROFIT & LOSS SUMMARY			
(ALL FIGURES ARE ANNUALIZED)			
PROJECTED SALES ($000)	358	1095	2040
COST OF SALES			
MATERIAL	182	600	1200
LABOR	47	150	300
OTHER COSTS			
OVERHEAD	82.5	82.5	100
ENGINEERING	12	30	40
ADMINISTRATION	51	51	60
SALES EXPENSE	30.5	40	50
TOTAL COST	405	953.5	1750
PROFIT CONTRIBUTION	(47)	141.5	290
LESS DEPRECIATION	36	50	75
PROFIT BEFORE TAX	(83)	91.5	215

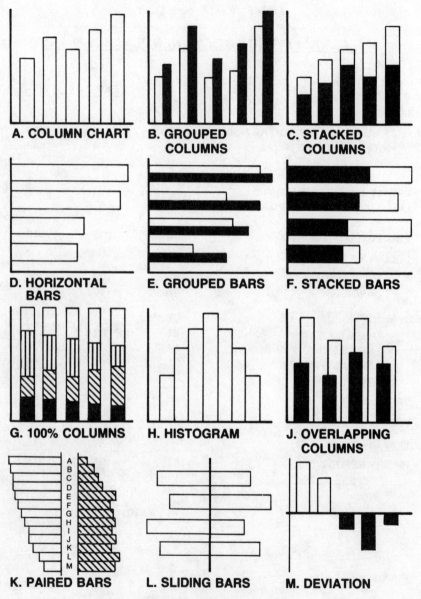

Figure 13 Using Bar Graphs

Grouped columns (B) and stacked columns (C) are used to show groups of related values over a time series. The two values shown in chart B, for example, might be cost of sales and sales income. With stacked columns, the amounts of the entire stacks must be more important than the relative size of the individual components. The reverse is true of grouped columns, where each component shares the same base line. For ease of interpretation, do not use more than three or four components per group or stack.

Horizontal bar charts (D) are used for comparing amounts and for showing differences among items. The order in which the bars are shown is up to you. There is no vertical scale. The label of each bar is entered at the left of the bar. Usually a time sequence is not involved; instead, you are comparing several things at one point in time. Grouped (E) and stacked (F) bars are used for the same reasons and with the same limitations as columns B and C.

The 100 percent columns chart (G) shows the relationship of the components to the whole over a time sequence or over varying conditions. Each column is the rectangular equivalent of a pie chart. As with stacked bars or stacked columns, the comparison of individual parts above the bottom "stack" is difficult. Thus, you should put the most important component on the bottom to share a common base line. Remember to keep the number of components to five or six at most. The bars should be shaded progressively lighter as they go upward.

The histogram (H) is used to show frequency distribution. Each bar shows how often that class occurs. Each class must be discrete, rather than continuous. For example, in the histogram in Figure 13, each column could represent the number of days needed to complete a shipment. The bars would be labeled "1 or Less, 2, 3, 4, 5, 6, and 7 or More."

Overlapping the columns (J) can be quite effective. It not only saves space, it can be used to emphasize the darker, shorter bars in the foreground. It is also useful in highlighting the differences in the amounts in each of the columns. Overlapping works well with horizontal bars too. One caution: This technique will work only if the bar in the background is always longer than the one in the foreground.

Paired bars (K) are used to show whether or not the relationship between two items follows a consistent pattern. Normally the bars of the independent variable are arranged in logical sequence (e.g., high to low) on the left. The dependent variable could show either a positive or negative correlation or no relationship at all.

Sliding bars (L) compare distinct groups by some common characteristic. For example, the number of smokers versus nonsmokers by age, by sex, by occupation, etc. Sliding bars are limited, because all the members of the group must fall on one or the other side of the center line—that is, all members must satisfy a yes/no, do/don't test, or this form of graphic won't work.

The deviation chart (M) shows differences from some value or goal. The value, often zero, is represented by the line from which the bars deviate. The line is horizontal in (M), but in many deviation charts the line is vertical.

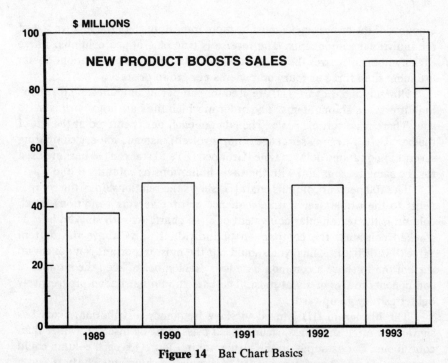

Figure 14   Bar Chart Basics

Some people prefer the latter arrangement because it provides more room for labeling the bars. Note that shading is used to highlight the negative values.

Figure 14 shows a basic bar chart. Look at it a bit more carefully. It also illustrates most of the basic rules for good design.

- All lettering should be horizontal.
- Use only one type style, preferably a sans serif typeface.
- Use at most only three type sizes.
- The largest type should be used for a title or headline that captures the main point of the visual. The headline should appear at the top and should be the same size for every visual.
- Vertical scale units should be at large tick marks only.
- Use heavy lines for the axes and the outlines of the bars.
- Use light lines for grid lines and the outer frame.
- Wherever possible avoid grid lines completely. Figure 14 has one only to illustrate the line thickness and the important point that guidelines are *not* drawn through bars.
- The space between the bars should be half the width of the bars.
- Omit zeros when the values are large.
- Avoid putting numbers inside or over the bars.

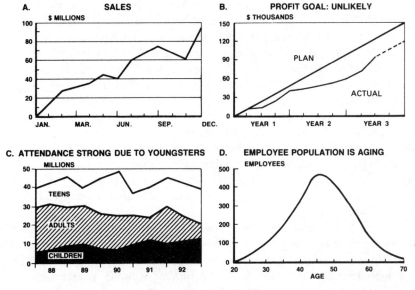

Figure 15 Line Graphs

- Label the units prominently at the top.
- If the bars contain several patterns, avoid using a legend. Instead label the patterns directly on one of the bars. Legends turn reading any chart into a two-step process.
- If a legend cannot be avoided, place it at or near the top—for example, under the title.
- The correct proportion for 35mm slides is two units high by three units wide.
- The correct size for overhead transparencies is 7¹/₂ inches high by 9¹/₂ inches wide.
- Avoid clutter!

Line Graphs

Line graphs are useful for showing a long series of data points. They are especially suited to showing changes over time. They emphasize trend line changes and movement. Figure 15 illustrates the use of a single- and a double-curve line chart (A and B), a surface chart (C), and a distribution chart (D).

Notice that heavy lines are used for the axes and the curves. The grid, when used, is made of thin lines. Graph A in Figure 15 has grid lines, but only to illustrate how they would look if you needed them for accurate reading.

The actual graph shown does not need grid lines. Graph B shows two curves. Note that they are both solid lines except the last part of the "Actual" curve. It is best to use solid lines for all curves if possible, labeling each curve clearly. Use dotted or dashed curves to show projections, plans, or estimates.

Surface graphs (or mountain graphs), such as Figure 15C, are best used to emphasize the individual and total *amounts* as well as the changes. As with bars, use darker shading at the bottom and make each higher surface progressively lighter. Place the labels within the surfaces wherever possible. If not, place them outside the graph to the right. As a last resort, use a legend. The least volatile curve should be placed at the bottom of the graph, with increasingly more irregular layers added as the graph goes higher. If all the layers are relatively smooth, place the most important, or the largest, component at the bottom. If the curves cross, use a different shading or color to show the area of overlap.

Frequency distributions (as in Figure 15D) are used to show whether the frequency of an occurrence is at the low end, the high end, or the center of a distribution, as shown. Of course, the frequency distribution of more than one population can be shown. Limit the number of curves in a frequency distribution to two or three, and limit the number of curves in other line graphs to four or five.

Pie Charts

Perhaps it's the fact that the circle suggests completeness that makes pie charts useful for showing the relative sizes of parts to a whole. Pie charts, or circle graphs, are used more often in business than in technical presentations, probably because of their limitations. For example, people perceive angular distances poorly; we tend to measure the areas of the sectors instead of comparing the degrees on the circle. One sector may be twice the size of another, and we may fail to realize it. Pie charts get messy if they use more than five or six sectors, which limits their use. Very small wedges (less than 3 percent) don't work well. Lastly, comparing component sectors of many pies is not as effective as using several bars.

Figure 16 shows a few variations on the pie theme. To determine how many degrees of arc to give each sector, multiply the percent of each component by 3.6 degrees. For example, a component which is 25 percent of the total will need 25 × 3.6 or 90 degrees of arc. Notice that the largest sector starts at twelve o'clock. The following sectors are in order of size. Shading or coloring should be different for each sector and should proceed from dark to light; the reverse will work, too. It's best to avoid leaving a sector blank; it tends to make it seem unimportant or even missing (except if the component *is missing*—then using a blank sector is a good way to highlight it). Place the label inside each sector if you have room. If not, place each label outside the

---

TECHNICAL COMPUTING

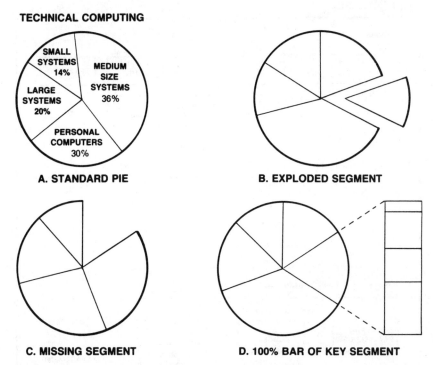

A. STANDARD PIE **B. EXPLODED SEGMENT**

C. MISSING SEGMENT **D. 100% BAR OF KEY SEGMENT**

Figure 16 Pie Chart Techniques

circle and as close to its sector as possible. Use arrows or leaders to connect each label with its sector. If necessary, show the value or the percent of each sector below the label.

The exploded segment is often used to emphasize a critical component. Note also the technique of further exploding the contents of the critical sector into a 100 percent bar. Note: if you use several pies, limit the number of sectors in each to three. Place them in the same sequence for each pie and be consistent as well with shading or coloring.

Diagrams and Schematics

Both can be useful for visuals in presentations. A *diagram* is a line drawing designed to explain rather than represent something (see Figure 17). Diagrams can be pictorial, showing only functional parts of a device, usually in a simplified way. They can also be verbal. In the block diagram, activities, operations, organizations, or parts of systems are represented by words inside rectangles and other shapes. *Schematics* show all the functional parts of a

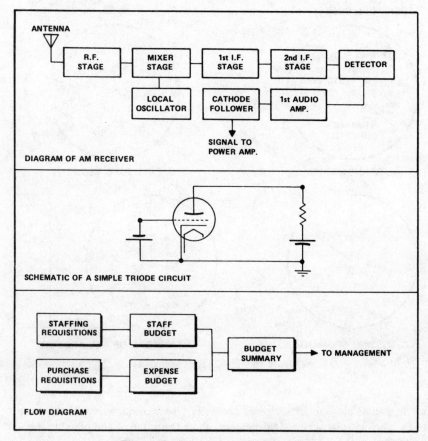

Figure 17 Diagrams and Schematics

device; they use conventional symbols to represent the parts. Diagrams are used extensively in technical presentations; schematics only occasionally.

Both diagrams and schematics present challenges as visuals. The closer the drawing gets to being a *working drawing,* the more unsuitable it becomes for use in a presentation. PERT diagrams (PERT: Program Evaluation and Review Technique, a program scheduling tool), or critical path diagrams, decision trees, and piping or wiring diagrams are *not* designed to be used as visuals; neither are electronic or pneumatic schematics or mechanical drawings. Some technical professionals have a tendency to use the output of CAD (Computer Aided Design) systems for visuals in presentations. No matter how technically astute the audience, this is decidedly a poor practice. The output is usually produced on a plotter and is too small for any but the smallest of audiences. What is far worse is the fact that such "drawings" contain masses of unnecessary and confusing lines.

Using Color

The effective use of color can greatly contribute to the success of a presentation, just as misuse of color can be a hindrance. Let's examine some of the facets of color, how best to use it, and some of the pitfalls to avoid.

We tend to respond to colors in different ways. For example, reds, oranges, and yellows give us a feeling of warmth, whereas greens, blues, and violets are considered cool colors. We perceive the warm hues to be closer; the cooler hues seem more distant. That is why it is best to use cool colors for background and warmer colors for foreground material in presentation visuals.

Beyond the general feeling of "warmth" or "coolness," we have much deeper associations and emotional responses to colors. The responses vary with individuals and even more so with different cultures. Here is a list of common associations with the basic colors for North American and European cultures:

Red

Excitement, tension, passion, blood, arousal, desire, vitality, impulsiveness, activity, fervor, hostility, anger, attack, courage, conquest, will to win, force of will, struggle, competition, vigor, masculinity, love, sexual stimulation, eroticism, danger, stop, fire, loss.

As you know, business people associate "red ink" with losses of all kinds. Since this color is associated with bad news, it should be used sparingly and only for emphasis in business presentations (unless you are dealing with real losses, of course).

Orange

Lively, exuberant, energetic, forceful, festive, funny, jovial, autumnal.

Yellow

Sunlight, brightness, heat, cheerful, jovial, welcoming, happy, vital, inspiring, hope, expansiveness, future-looking, adventure, sacred, god, creation, holy, celestial, relaxation, volatility, change, piquancy, caution.

Green

Nature, abundance, earth, trees, country, spring, fresh, quiet, relaxing, tranquil, cool, peaceful, refreshing, self-preservation, perseverance, pride, self-esteem, control, youth, power, hope.

Blue

Water, sky, sea, ice, calmness, tranquility, quiet, serenity, peace, thoughtfulness, contemplative, reflection, meditative, cold, subdued, sober, order, spiritual, piety, sincerity, integrity, fidelity, loyalty, truth, trust, security, comfort, soothing, contentment, fulfillment, police, navy, men, melancholy.

When North Americans are asked to name their favorite color, the most frequent answer is blue. Red comes in a close second.

Violet

Wish fulfillment, magical, mystical, emotional insecurity, unrealistic, impractical.

Purple

Dignity, splendor, mysticism, power, wealth, cool, mourning.

Brown

Rich, earth, roots, body sensations, ease, comfort, physical contentment, security, sensory satisfaction, neutral.

Gray

Somber, quietness, conservative, dignity, age, non-involvement, neutral.

White

Purity, innocence, virginal, clean, frank, youthful, spirited, zest, the beginning. marriages, peace, cool, hospitals, sterile, yes.

To illustrate the cultural influences on our reactions to color, note that we associate youth, marriages, and the beginnings of things with white. In Japan, white is a funereal color, associated with death.

Black

Emptiness, nothingness, death, extinction, the end, relinquishment, mourning, gloomy, sorrowful, depressing, evil, ominous, deadly, no.

Think carefully about the likely response your audience will have to your color selection. Analysis of your audience should influence your choice of colors. A very young audience generally responds best to bright reds, oranges, and yellows. More mature audiences resonate more with blue, green, and white.

The entry of computers into presentations has caused a profusion of color. Resist the temptation to use color for purely decorative purposes. Use it instead for *functional* ends. For example:

- Text slides should consist of no more than two colors, with the possible use of a third, bright color for occasional touches of emphasis.
- Use color to show which elements of the visual are more important than the rest. For example, use the same cool color for three of the four lines in a line chart, and show the fourth—and most important—line with a bright, warm color.
- Use color thematically to identify different functions, elements or levels of importance in the visual.
- Limit the number of colors in any visual to three or four.
- Be consistent in your use of color throughout the entire presentation.
- Choose colors that look attractive together. Avoid garish color clash.
- One of the most popular choices for text slides is white or yellow letters on a background of deep blue. In fact, deep blue is the most popular color for business presentations.
- For 35mm slides, use warm, bright hues in the foreground, cooler colors or neutral shades in the background. The reverse is true for overhead transparencies, for which backgrounds should be light, white, or transparent and foregrounds darker.
- Avoid the overuse of bright, fully saturated colors; they tend to overpower the data you are trying to show.
- Avoid mixing red and green. People with color blindness will have difficulty interpreting the visual.
- Neutral gray is especially effective as a background color.
- Crimson works well as a foreground color with gray backgrounds.

Use color carefully: It can highlight vital elements, attract and hold attention, improve clarity, and even improve memorability.

VISUALS FOR TECHNICAL PRESENTATIONS

The challenge in making visuals for technical presentations is to provide a level of detail that will help the audience focus on your message and prevent them from exploring the wonderful intricacies and technical details they may see before them. All of the characteristics of effective visuals apply to technical presentations. The problem is that these characteristics are usually harder to achieve, especially *simplicity, readability, and clarity.* Here are some ideas for producing effective visuals for technical presentations:

- Use simple diagrams to give an overview of your subject, then explain the details one by one with *separate* visuals.
- Plan each visual so that you will speak to it for about 2 minutes.
- If you must show a large, complex diagram (or schematic), do it in stages. Begin by showing parts of the diagram that relate to each other functionally, then progressively build to the final diagram by adding more visuals. Of course, this works only if the diagram or schematic lends itself to being explained area by area. Usually it is possible to lay it out in a way that makes progressive building possible.
- Instead of a series of "build" transparencies, consider overlays. Up to three transparencies can be made to be placed on top of the first.
- With 35mm slides, the diagram can be photographed as each stage is added, thus producing the same gradual buildup.
- Use schematics only if every member of your audience is familiar with the symbols.
- Do not use working documents for visuals.
- Always keep the audience in mind. What can be done to make the visual simple, clear, and arresting for this particular audience?

Pictures (35mm slides) add interest, color, and realism to any presentation. In a technical presentation, they are useful for showing what the object looks like, but not for showing how it works. Photographs usually show too much detail and too many nonfunctional parts to be useful by themselves in a technical exposition. (Imagine trying to learn how an internal combustion engine works by looking at pictures of engines and engine parts.) Use diagrams to explain function in tandem with photographs to show appearance, size, and location.

For expository purposes, technical illustrations have two big advantages over photographs. Technical illustrations do not show unimportant detail and they can cut away the outside to reveal and highlight the functioning parts within.

Models and mockups may be useful adjuncts to technical presentations. A scale model of the technical device can help to explain the features and principles of operation of the real device, especially if the model operates. One reason for using a model or mockup is that the real object cannot be brought into the room. Another is that the real object does not yet exist.

Models and mockups are unusual in business and technical presentations because they are expensive to produce. The expense must be justified by the stakes (as with an architectural model for a new building) or by the fact that the presentation will be given repeatedly to a very large number of people. Another limiting factor is that the size of the model or mockup usually limits its use to small audiences. This limitation can be overcome in part, however, by using 35mm slides of the model from every important viewing angle.

Technical professionals involved in the development and design of new products are aware that the use of models to show the appearance and test the performance of new products is commonplace. In such technical organizations, the use of models or photographs of them is also commonplace.

GETTING HELP

Planning, designing, and producing visuals are skills that one learns by doing. Each frame presents a different challenge. No two solutions are alike, and each new solution produces new learning. To help quicken your learning, seek the advice and assistance of the specialists in your organization or even of an audiovisual design firm if the stakes are high enough to justify the expense.

9

Consider the Physical Factors

One common mistake speakers make is ignoring the purely physical elements of a presentation. Yet it is almost impossible to communicate with another human being without satisfying at least a threshold level of physical comfort. For example, an audience cannot concentrate its attention for long periods unless the room temperature is within a narrow range (about 68 to 75° F). The presentation *itself* is, after all, a purely physical act.

The objective of this chapter is to help you become sensitive to the physical aspects of audience communication so that you can avoid distractions and heighten your audience's ability to absorb your message. We begin with the environment.

THE ROOM

The location of the presentation has a direct bearing on your audience's ability to concentrate on your material. At best it can be a neutral factor. At worst, the room can make communication all but impossible. If you can exercise control over the presentation room, by all means do so. Here is a checklist to help you choose a room that won't derail your presentation.

The *temperature* is most critical, as mentioned. Avoid at all costs rooms that are too hot. Few things can annoy, distract, and stupefy an audience more than a warm, humid room. Select a room that is on the cool side (68° F). People can get warm by putting on more clothing, but social norms severely limit the extent to which one may disrobe in public. If the room seems a bit too cool at first, be patient. Each member of your audience is a small furnace, generating heat that warms the room.

The *size* is important, too. Rooms that are too small can create acute discomfort for people who need a large bubble of personal space around them. Rooms that are vastly oversized can create an eerie, vault-like effect.

The *shape* of the room influences both a speaker's ability to make contact with the members of the audience and their ability to see, hear, and communicate with each other. Generally, it is wise to avoid long, narrow rooms. They usually require you to overpower the people in front in order to reach those at the rear of the room. Moreover, people must lean and crane their necks to see you and the screen. Long, narrow rooms can inhibit discussion among you and audience members. The sad truth is most business and technical presentations are held in conference rooms—long, narrow rooms better suited for meetings than presentations. If you can, choose a room that is square, or nearly so. Square rooms allow the audience to see the speaker and the screen more easily, and the speaker is more able to move about freely. Square rooms allow for much more flexibility in seating your audience as well.

Check the *acoustics*. If the room is acoustically too absorbent (heavy drapes, thick rugs, acoustic-tiled ceilings, padded furniture), your voice will be soaked up like water pouring over dry sand. You will have to shout to be heard by everyone. In 10 minutes your voice will have become a raspy whisper. At the opposite extreme is the room that is so acoustically bright or reflective that the reverberations bouncing off the hard walls actually compete with the direct sound of your voice. Is the room so large, or the acoustics so poor that you will need to use a public address system?

If you need to use a *microphone*, follow these few tips. The best choice of microphone is a *wireless* mike that clips to your lapel or blouse (not a hand-held wireless mike). The small transmitter pack clips to the belt or fits in a large pocket. This microphone allows you to move around the room without being concerned about tripping on or pulling wires, and you won't have to worry about the mike being too far from your mouth. Second best choice is a lapel or lavaliere (neck) microphone. This type does keep the mike at the same distance from your mouth no matter what you do, but you must become adept at managing (not tripping over) the cord. The third and least desirable type is the fixed microphone, commonly attached to the top surface of lecterns, or on stands. Avoid fixed microphones. Using them requires a great deal of skill. You must constantly keep your mouth at the same distance from a fixed mike or the volume will fade. This severely restricts head and body movements. In effect, you become a prisoner of the microphone. Whatever kind you use, make sure the volume and tone controls are set correctly before your presentation. This is especially important for preventing *acoustic feedback,* the all-too-familiar howling, squealing sound that develops when sound from the loudspeaker feeds back into the microphone, creating a sound return loop that builds to ear shattering proportions.

Air circulation is vital in a presentation room. Without adequate circulation, your audience will be even more annoyed than usual over smoke or the odors that accompany stale air.

Light dimming capability is crucial if you intend to show 35mm slides or movies. A common mistake is to extinguish the lights entirely. Deprived of visual stimuli, many audience members simply fall asleep. Choose a room in which the lights can be dimmed just enough to enable your audience to see the 35mm slides clearly, and to take notes should they wish to.

The arrangement of the chairs and the speaker's space is especially important. Place the speaker so that no distractions, such as windows or doors, are nearby or behind.

A poorly arranged room can have a devastating effect on a presentation. Such an instance occurred recently when a corporation invited a college professor, who is a renowned expert in his field, to lecture to a group of company employees. The speaker had flown 1,500 miles to speak in a room that looked like the one diagrammed in Figure 18. The professor was scheduled to speak from 1:30 to 3:00 P.M. He began at about 1:35. A seemingly endless procession of latecomers was forced to walk directly in front of the speaker to enter the room.

After 10 minutes of constant interruption, the professor ran out of funny lines to comment on the late arrivals and his predicament. The last straggler entered the room at 2:50—10 minutes before the presentation was supposed to end! The occasion was a monumental disaster. If someone had considered the physical arrangement of the room, the results could have been quite different (see Figure 19).

With this arrangement, the inevitable latecomers could have taken their seats without distracting either the professor or the audience.

ARRANGING THE SEATS AND AUDIOVISUAL EQUIPMENT

Give careful attention to the seating and screen placement. Most important, be sure everyone in the room can see the visuals. Figure 20 suggests four of many acceptable arrangements.

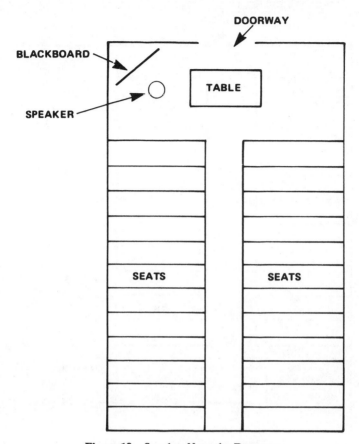

Figure 18 Speaker Near the Doorway

The overhead projector works best with the screen set at an angle to the audience. The image can be viewed clearly at fairly steep angles, as much as 30 degrees from the plane of the screen. Use a beaded screen for the widest viewing angle.

If the screen in the room is permanently fixed and parallel to the audience (as is most often the case), you have a problem with the overhead projector. Your body, and perhaps the overhead projector itself, will block the view of several audience members. This is one of the most common—and most annoying—mistakes made by inexperienced presenters. Several strategies can be used to ensure everyone will be able to see the visuals:

- Before the audience arrives, move the chairs that give an obstructed view of the screen.

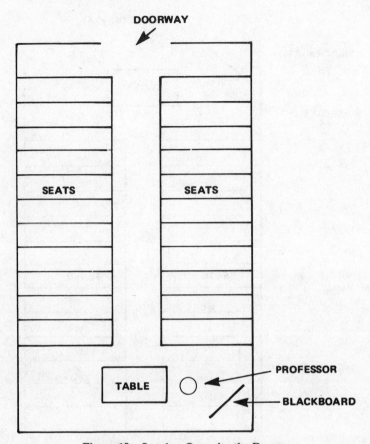

Figure 19   Speaker Opposite the Doorway

- If moving chairs is insufficient, do not stand next to the projector during the presentation. Instead, move next to the screen. Stand where everyone can see your visuals. Get your cues by glancing at the screen. Another technique is to make photocopies of your visuals with an office copier. Use the photocopies as slip sheets to separate the transparencies. During the presentation, hold the photocopy of the visual being projected in your hand and glance down at it to get your cues.
- If nothing else will work, as a last resort, seat yourself next to the projector. Speaking to an audience while seated is generally to be avoided. It is extremely difficult to establish any presence and audience contact from a seated position. The one exception to this advice occurs when your audience is so small (one to four) that by standing you overpower them.

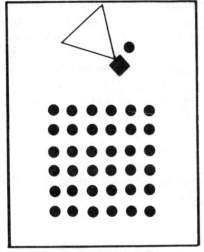

A. AUDITORIUM STYLE WITH
OVERHEAD PROJECTOR

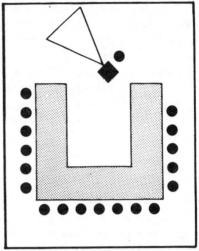

B. CONFERENCE STYLE WITH
OVERHEAD PROJECTOR

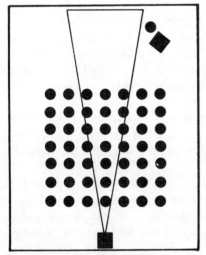

C. AUDITORIUM STYLE WITH
35mm PROJECTOR

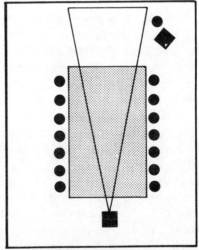

D. CONFERENCE STYLE WITH
35mm PROJECTOR

Figure 20   Typical Room Arrangements

The 35mm projector can be used with the screen parallel to the audience, as shown in Figures 20C and 20D, or it can be used at an angle. Be sure to *raise* the 35mm projector high enough to project over the heads of your audience. Special tables with telescoping legs are available for this purpose. Raise the screen as high as possible, too. Always place projectors where the heat and noise from their blowers will not annoy or distract anyone.

Some conference or presentation rooms, especially those in hotels, use a whiteboard for both writing and as a projector screen. Whiteboards make poor screens; they are almost always too small, and they produce a hot spot in the center, where high reflectivity of the projector beam makes the visual unreadable. Ask the facility function manager for a real screen.

Notice the location of the speaker in the diagrams in Figure 20. With the screen at an angle to the audience, it is easier to stand next to the overhead projector without blocking anyone's view of the visuals. The table on which the projector sits should be large enough to hold the visuals and whatever else the speaker needs, such as a pointer, a pitcher of water, and a glass.

Incidentally, the best way to point with overhead transparencies is with a pen or pencil. Place it on the transparency with the point under the part you wish to highlight.

With 35mm slides, stand next to the screen and face the audience. A lectern or table is placed nearby for your notes and other needs.

Lecterns can become traps. Most inexperienced presenters stand behind them, clutching the sides of the lectern in a death grip, staring down at their notes, largely ignoring their audience. But if you have designed your visuals properly, you will not need to read from notes. Your cues will be on the screen. If you do plan to use a lectern, use it as a reference table.

The best place to stand with 35mm presentations is next to the screen. Have a pointer in the hand closer to the screen. Point directly on the screen to the items you wish to highlight. And in the other hand, hold the switch for advancing your slides.

Use a wooden or telescoping metal pointer. The optical type—the kind that projects a beam of light, usually in the form of an arrow—is hard to control. The arrow leaps and darts about the screen, seemingly with a life of its own. Most audience members are fascinated with the pointer, to the exclusion of everything else on the screen.

Plan to control your own slides, rather than use an assistant. By being in control yourself, you can project the next slide exactly when you want it and on precisely the words you choose. Using an assistant can introduce awkward delays, because your helper must be utterly certain you have finished with the current slide. Premature changes can also occur when you choose to say just a bit more than you usually do with a slide. Lastly, the use of a confederate can lead to awkward exchanges, such as, "Next slide, please" or "Could you go back to the last slide, Fred?"

For nonprojected media (easel pads, flipcharts), place the visuals as close to the audience as possible without blocking anyone's view. For large groups, the nonprojected visual should be raised so that people sitting in back can see them.

The *chairs* should be comfortable. One maker of folding chairs has designed a hard metal chair that perennially wins the "Iron Maiden" award for exquisite discomfort. The back of the chair slices audience members just above the kidneys. Avoid uncomfortable chairs if possible, especially when your presentation is a long one. Be sure that you have provided enough chairs (regardless of the kind) to seat your entire audience. It is distracting to have people wandering about seeking chairs once you have begun your presentation.

Check the number and locations of *electrical outlets*. Will you need extension cords to operate your equipment? Some facilities, especially the older, "quaint" ones still have two-prong electrical outlets. You will need a special adapter in order to plug in modern, three-prong equipped projectors.

Distractions of any kind can ruin a presentation. Over the years, I have had to cope with banging pipes, traffic (vehicular, airplane, and human), a man felling and trimming a tree with a chainsaw, clinking plates and silverware from a cafeteria, kitchen noises, ringing telephones, the sounds of movies, cheering crowds in adjacent rooms, the roar of air conditioning units, jackhammers—the list is interminable. Some distractions are unforeseeable. Nonetheless, it is still crucial to examine the presentation environment thoughtfully and to select a setting that is as free from distractions as possible.

Now that you have selected and prepared the best possible room, let's bring some people into it.

WHAT TIME?

As with selecting and arranging the room, if you can choose the time of your presentation, by all means do so. Choose a time when your audience is most likely to be physically ready and mentally alert. I recently asked a group what was the worst day of the week to attend a presentation. One wag responded, "Sunday!" Most people agree that in a *normal* work week, Monday mornings and Friday afternoons are the worst times. Another time to avoid is immediately after lunch. The body seems to respond to the task of processing food more readily than to processing ideas. Incidentally, if you have any influence over the menu, plan for a light meal and do not include alcoholic beverages.

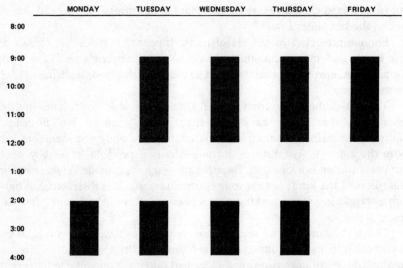

Figure 21   Optimum Times for Presentations

Less serious, but still worth avoiding are early morning or late afternoon presentations. Some of us are slow starters (the evening or night people), and those who are not (the morning people) are likely to have lost that sharp edge by 4:00 P.M. Figure 21 is a chart showing the ideal times to conduct presentations. Of course, one cannot always achieve perfection, but if you can choose the time, choose one that will enhance your chances of success.

HOW LONG?

What is the limit of an audience's physical endurance? I must thank Professor Brian Quinn of Dartmouth College for introducing me to the term *Fanny Factor.* (The brain can absorb only as much as the fanny can.) But there is also an attention-span factor, a lack-of-body-movement factor, a thirst factor, a hunger factor, and, the most pressing of all, the bladder factor. These limitations to the human machine dictate an absolute limit of about 1¼ to 1½ hours. Beyond that, people will begin to get up and leave the room, and those that remain will have departed mentally. If at all possible, limit your presentation to one hour. If it will take much longer than 60 minutes to cover your material, give people a short break after the first hour.

On the subject of breaks, have you ever thought which break is the most important during the day? Of course, it's the first one in the morning. The reason? Coffee. We preface our meetings with cups of coffee—one of nature's most powerful diuretics. Then we expect people to remain in their seats for two hours! Have mercy.

Audiences will tell you when they need a break. Look for the signs: bored (or anxious) facial expressions, "slouchy" posture, a physical sense of distraction, withdrawal gestures (such as glancing at watches or staring at the floor), shuffling feet, even a kind of dreamy lassitude can signal it is time to stop and recharge batteries.

THE OTHER EQUIPMENT

Of course, you will not forget to have a projector in the room, but what other equipment will you need? Here is a checklist of other equipment and related items:

3-prong adapter
Audiovisual assistant (for emergencies)
Backup projector
Blackboard
Blackboard eraser
Chalk
Duct tape (to tape cords to the floor)
Easel
Easel pad
Easel pad marker
Extension cords (electrical)
Extension for 35mm advancing switch
Flip charts
Grease pencil
Handouts
Lectern
Masking tape (2″ wide)
PA system
Pointer
Screen
Slides
Spare fuses
Spare projector bulbs
Table for projector

You should always plan to arrive early. Make sure the projection equipment is set up, focused, and operating properly. Go through all the visuals to ensure they are in correct order and none is positioned upside down or backwards. Then check to ensure that you and your audience will have everything you both will need.

OTHER NECESSITIES

Here is a checklist of items not related to equipment but equally important (some are optional):

    3-by-5-inch cards for jotting down questions
    A copy of the agenda
    Chairs (arranged properly)
    Coffee
    Decaffeinated coffee
    Fruit
    Fruit juice
    Pastries
    Name tags
    Pencils
    Place cards
    Soft drinks
    Tables that will allow them to write
    Tea
    Water for them
    Water for you
    Writing pads for their notes

REMEMBER MURPHY

Much of the physical side of presentations is basic, commonsense planning. But the subject is no less crucial for its simplicity, because communication is both a physical and a mental process. And the mental part cannot work without the physical component. We reach each other through intellectual and logical channels, through emotional channels, and, at the root, through our physical senses. Plan that physical dimension as carefully as you would any other part of the presentation.

One final piece of advice: When it comes to physical considerations, never take chances and never take anything for granted. Murphy's Law states: "Whatever can go wrong . . . will."

As we now know, Murphy was an optimist.

10

Deliver Your Presentation

We have arrived at the final plateau. All of the thinking, planning, organizing, writing, choosing, designing, visual production—all the preparation has led to this, the *physical act* of communicating with your audience.

Delivering a presentation requires that you use your body to convey information and ideas, that you use it so that the focus of the audience is centered on the message, not on you. But you cannot be merely a passive transmission device. Audiences view your material as an extension of *you*. They are just as interested in getting a sense of you as they are in receiving your message. Your goal as a presenter is not only to intensify your audience's awareness of your subject with a minimum of distractions, but also to communicate a positive sense of *you* as well.

WHAT IS SO DIFFICULT?

Speaking to an audience can have some spooky effects on some people. Bright, warm, articulate men and women who are confident and outgoing in private conversations suddenly undergo complete personality changes when

129

they must speak to a group. They become awed by the audience, shy, introverted, awkward, and uncomfortable. They stare at the floor, hide their hands, or use them to clutch or fiddle with objects. They speak too quietly, too quickly, or haltingly, or in rapid, machine-gun bursts, usually in voices devoid of vitality and animation. In short, they become strangers. The first goals of this chapter are to explore the causes underlying this mysterious malady and to provide some preventive medicine. From there, we will explore the characteristics of effective delivery and the specific skills that will help you communicate more naturally and more confidently with audiences.

The purpose of this chapter is not to transform you into another Clarence Darrow or Demosthenes; the aim is simply to help you use the communication skills you acquired as a child, along with the physical and mental equipment you possess as an adult, in order to speak effectively and competently with audiences as *yourself*, without feeling apprehensive or having unreasonable expectations.

THE QUEST FOR PERFECTION

Probably the most unreasonable expectation is that we must be perfect. We must represent the highest form, the most advanced development of our species. Not one mispronounced word, not one imperfect gesture, not a cough or a single "um" is permissible.

Perhaps because most of the speakers we see on television seem perfect (most of the time), we have come to expect a standard of excellence far beyond what is realistic. Television performers wear makeup, have professional lighting and set designers, and most crucially, have teleprompters to tell them exactly what to say. The visual channel is operated by a team of professionals in a control room. To expect such perfection in everyday business or technical presentations is not only unrealistic, it is genuinely destructive.

If we seek perfection, we program ourselves for failure. No one is perfect, certainly not for very long. Sooner or later one of our imperfections has to reveal itself. When that happens, and all the world (at least the part we care about) knows that we are imperfect, how will we react? Reactions range from mild distress and discomfort all the way to disorientation and even "freezing."

Trying to be perfect causes us to use elaborately detailed notes, so that every word will be exactly the one intended, and not even the subtlest of nuances will be lost. (This often leads to the awkward practice of reading notes to the audience.) Trying to be perfect can cause us to seem ill-at-ease, or simply to give the impression that we are trying too hard.

Audiences are far less sensitive to our imperfections than we are ourselves. Most audiences tend to ignore or accept them unless they become distracting. In fact an occasional slip can reassure them that you too are human. Being imperfect helps you to establish a relationship with your audience.

TRYING TO BE SOMEONE ELSE

In workshops, I often hear comments like this: "I have known John for 10 years and somehow he seemed different during his presentation. His voice was different. He seemed much more subdued and low-key than he always is. He did things with his hands I have never seen him do before. He didn't look at us. He just wasn't John."

Early in life we seem to acquire the tendency to be somebody else when giving a presentation. Have you ever seen a child recite a poem for a visiting relative? The voice becomes little Johnny's (and little everybody's) stilted, sing-songy "recitation" voice. Little Johnny stands with legs crossed, eyes fixed on the ceiling, an apprehensive look on his face, hands clasped behind his back, his whole body rocking back and forth or twisting awkwardly. When the recitation is over and Aunt Martha applauds energetically, Johnny becomes a real child again, his natural posture, facial expressions, voice, and movements now in striking contrast to that of his recitation person.

As adults, many of us never quite outgrow our recitation behavior. True, we are more subtle than little Johnny. We have much more grown up ways to demonstrate our recitation person. Unfortunately, those habits still interfere with effective audience communication.

One of the most frequent pieces of advice given to people seeking to improve their "public speaking" is *be yourself.* This is good advice, but like the tips "don't worry" or "relax," it is sometimes hard to follow. Here are a few thoughts that can help give you the confidence to *present yourself* to audiences.

One of my clients once said that in delivering an extremely important presentation he put on the best "Orson Welles imitation" he could muster. I hastened to tell him that imitating another speaker's style is not a good idea. The best one can hope for is a second-rate Orson Welles or Winston Churchill. What is needed is a first-rate *you.* The audience wants to get a sense of who *you* are, of what *your* style is like.

Try to forget the notions that you have to be special when you speak before a group of people or that you must impress your audience. This frame of mind will bring out your recitation person, not the real you.

OVERALL RULES FOR EFFECTIVE DELIVERY

Rule One: Engagement

Question: If you could reduce delivery skill to one word, what would that word be?

Answer: Delivery skill cannot be reduced to one word, but the word that comes closest is *engagement*. Engagement means reaching out to make contact with your audience. It means coming forward and meeting an audience the way you would meet anyone you wish to get to know. *Engagement means establishing a relationship with an audience.*

One of the difficulties for the inexperienced or infrequent speaker is making the audience feel comfortable. If the speaker, somewhat overawed by the audience, seems uneasy, the audience will mirror that feeling. This reflection tends to make the presenter even *more* uncomfortable, and the process begins to feed on itself! How many speakers have you seen who withdraw to the extent that they seem not to want to be in the room? How did that make *you* feel?

If you work to engage an audience, they know it; it shows in your face, your voice, your movements. Your audience, for their part, will reflect your efforts as positive feedback. They will show it in *their* faces, posture and movements. The relationship you have established creates a kind of resonance among everyone in the room.

Rule Two: Energy

Listening is hard work, requiring the spending of a huge amount of total energy by the audience. A skillful speaker must work as hard at delivering as the audience does at listening. In fact, the speaker should match the total energy output expected of the audience. The energy flows outward from your voice, face, eyes—from your entire body.

If the speaker's energy level is low, the whole delivery takes on a subdued, lackluster, "ho-hum" quality. The voice is soft and flat. The face and eyes lack vitality and expression. The body seems passive. In this low-energy state, you can make the most thrilling statements and the audience will still reflect boredom and disengagement.

Energy does not mean enthusiasm, although that's part of it. After all, as Dale Carnegie observed many years ago, if you are not enthusiastic about your subject, how can you expect your audience to be? But energy is more than enthusiasm, it is an intensity—a vitality—that you project and transmit to your audience. They sense that you are *working* at reaching them.

You are the power source that makes the presentation go.

Rule Three: Empathy

Earlier in this book we discussed analyzing your audience. Once you have a profile of your audience, it should influence every step that follows. Delivery is no exception.

A skilled presenter is *audience-centered,* not *self-centered.* Empathy is the ability to *become* your audience, to be able to think what they are thinking, to imagine what it is like to be sitting out there experiencing your presentation. Audiences sense when a speaker is involved with them, and they respond to it. By focusing your mental energies on your audience you will create a rapport with them. You will also avoid the pitfalls that accompany self-centeredness. You will be asking mental questions such as:

Can that woman in the back row hear me?
Does he understand this point?
Are they getting tired?
Can this person up front see the whole screen?
Is the pace too fast (or slow)?
Does he have a question?
Does she agree?
Do they need a break?

You will *not* be asking yourself destructive questions such as:

Do they like me?
Am I doing well?
Can they tell how nervous I am?
Is my tie straight?
Can they see my missing button?
Will I make a mistake?

Questions like those in the latter group cannot help but detract from the effectiveness of your delivery.

The presenter who has empathy is constantly looking and listening for audience feedback. Facial expressions, movements, gestures, sounds, eye contact, posture—all are messages. If you are in tune with your audience, you will be sensitive to these nonverbal cues and will respond to them by changing your pace, asking a question, asking if any of them has a question, stopping for a break, or doing whatever seems an appropriate response to the unspoken messages you are receiving.

Impact on Delivery

Engagement, energy, and empathy are interlocking elements in the process of audience communication. When one or more of these elements is missing, the impact on delivery is predictable; the speaker:

- Has little or no eye contact
- Speaks too fast with few or no pauses
- Speaks too softly
- Has a voice with no vitality or dynamism
- Does not move (or moves incessantly)
- Displays distracting mannerisms
- Seems ill-at-ease or uncomfortable
- Doesn't establish a rapport with the audience

Engagement, energy, and empathy together help you to produce the opposite results, a smooth and animated vocal delivery, body posture and movements that are natural, and, perhaps most important of all, a manner that makes your audience sense that you are happy to be with them.

But all this can still be suddenly lost if you are not ready to invoke Rule Four when needed.

Rule Four: Keep Going

Disaster awaits you.

Sorry, but it's on your schedule. If you give enough presentations, sooner or later something has to go wrong. The screen will roll up with a clatter; the projector bulb will blow; the building will lose power; you will say something that is incorrect, ill-conceived, or embarrassing; you will massacre a word; you will lose your place; someone in your audience will help you by discovering and pointing out a misspelled word in one of your visuals; you will totally forget what you want to say; a visual will be projected upside down, backwards, or out of sequence; you will suddenly realize that you have earlier omitted information or given incorrect information. . . . There's more, but the more squeamish among you must be spared the gruesome details.

One of the most valuable and helpful ideas you can take from this book is *no matter what happens, keep going.*

Be mentally prepared for disruptions, mistakes, and accidents. When something goes wrong:

- Don't panic.
- Don't freeze.
- Don't apologize.
- Don't get flustered.
- Don't excuse yourself.
- Don't humiliate yourself.
- Don't poke derisive fun at yourself.
- Don't think that the wrath of god has descended upon you for all your past sins, your lack of preparation, or your general cussedness. These things happen to everybody.

- Don't "break" (step outside your role as presenter and comment on the situation, the presentation, or your performance).
- Don't call further attention to the problem by highlighting it.
- Don't stop unless you must. Try not to lose momentum.
- Do take whatever action is necessary to restore normalcy without creating more of a disruption.
- If you have equipment breakdowns, set to work to fix or replace the equipment. You need not suddenly become an entertainer to fill in the time. Simply ask for a few moments, or, *if it's appropriate,* take a break.

Few things make one cringe as much as human beings humiliating themselves because a slide is out of place. If you have a cough on the day of the presentation, does it help your audience to concentrate if you say "excuse me" every time you cough? Does it really help your image if, after making a mistake, you "break" by saying, "nice going, dummy"?

One of the most useful things to remember is that *the audience doesn't know anything about your presentation.* They have to discover everything! If you accidentally put a visual on the screen out of its intended order, *you are the only person in the room who knows that.* Why let everybody else know?

"Oh, I'm terribly sorry. This slide was meant to introduce the last three topics I covered. I guess somehow I must have inserted it in the wrong place when I was going over the visuals last night. Yesterday was a long day. . . ."

Should this happen to you, either take the offending slide off the screen without comment, or—better—use it in some inventive way:

"And, to summarize, these were the last three topics we have covered."

Another variation on the theme that the audience doesn't know about your presentation . . . suppose you have to give a presentation with almost no time to prepare (it happens). Will it help your cause if you begin your presentation as follows:

"Good morning. I just want you to know that I haven't had the usual amount of time to prepare for this presentation. So as I go through this, I hope you will bear in mind that this is not up to my usual standards."

How about this for a beginning:

"Good afternoon. I hope you will excuse my voice. I am just getting over a terrible cold. I'm having a good deal of difficulty talking."

The one thing you can now be sure of is the audience will be 10 times more aware of every imperfection in your voice than would have been the case had you not mentioned it.

Another trap to avoid is the *damaging editorial comment.* In this case, the speaker inserts just a little aside in passing:

"Now that I have totally confused you . . ."
"Maybe I have said this before."
"I'm going to cover—probably too early . . ."
"I probably didn't do a good job setting the stage for this."
"This may sound somewhat innocuous."

In all these and similar cases, if the audience may be getting less than an ideal presentation, *let them discover that for themselves.* This is a far better course than casting a pall over the entire presentation at the outset and highlighting some imperfection that may otherwise go unnoticed. A good practice to follow is *never apologize.* And, by all means, never *begin* with an apology.

Granted, every decade or two something cataclysmic might require you to stop your presentation. Earthquakes, tornados, and hurricanes come to mind. Short of that class of show-stopper, be mentally prepared to deal with disruptions and imperfections. Don't be overwhelmed or derailed.

Keep going!

Rule Five: Manage Your Nervous Energy

After speaking before audiences for over 20 years, I am still nervous when I begin to speak to a new group. In fact, virtually everyone is nervous at first when speaking to an audience—even seasoned, professional performers. The signs are subtle, but if you look for them you can tell when a performer, for example, is working off the itchies and finally arrives at the stabilization point—the point when the performer settles into him or herself—where the nervous energy becomes unobtrusive and productive. The bad news is that you can always expect to be a bit nervous, and this book can't make the butterflies go away.

But *energy*, remember, is vital to effective speaking; good delivery requires heaps of it. The *good* news is that you can harness that primal and potentially destructive nervous energy and use it in productive ways. You can use its power to establish your "presence" and to reach your audience. If you speak to audiences often enough, you will come to realize that you need that energy. You will discover more of its secrets, too; the most important is that nervous energy can be managed.

Let's look first at the physical side of nervousness, then examine the frame of mind that usually causes the problem.

All the Wrong Things

It is curious how unharnessed nervous energy makes us do everything wrong. Breathing is usually the first thing affected. It becomes shallower and more rapid than normal. This causes most people to speak too softly and too quickly, often in bursts. We begin to stumble over our words. In extreme cases, the voice quavers. Our bodies get a bit low on oxygen, causing us to sigh every few minutes. Our saliva and mucus secretions shut down, causing our mouths to get dry, sometimes so dry that the audience can hear the sound of the tongue separating from the palate as we speak. The most important tool we have for making contact with our audience—the voice—is usually the first casualty.

But not always. On rare occasions the mind goes blank. It is not that we cannot think; we just cannot think of what we want to say. When this happens to beginners, they usually freeze, which induces an even deeper mental paralysis.

The entire body responds to the increased flow of adrenaline. The energy boiling within seeks escape. The heart rate increases, so does respiration. The hands clutch at or fuss with objects (pencils, pointers), with parts of clothing (rings, buttons, neckties, bracelets, earrings, eyeglasses), or the hands go to war with each other, pulling, twisting, and squeezing one another in a battle for supremacy. Muscles get so tight they quiver. Our hands shake. Some of us react to the energy by pacing ceaselessly or doing a perpetual little box step if we are short of space. Others stand ramrod straight, every muscle taut, as if we were facing a firing squad. We appear ill-at-ease, uncomfortable—even in pain. We convey the impression that what we want most is to get it over with. These are the normal reactions of a body preparing to deal with danger. Everybody has them to a greater or lesser extent, and everybody can learn to control them.

What Are You Afraid Of?

Let's talk about *fear*. If you wish, use a softer word. Why are you (concerned) (apprehensive) (worried) (uneasy) (anxious) (troubled)? Take your choice, nervousness is a primal response to a primal—and normal—emotion: fear. The vast majority of people in all walks of life *dread* having to speak in public. Indeed, *The Book of Lists, Number One* reports that Americans rank "speaking before a group" as their number one fear.* They dread it more than death itself (which is a mere seventh on the list). When someone says, "I'd rather *die* than speak in front of an audience," apparently they really mean it!

We react to fear in one of two ways: either by standing our ground and fighting or by running away from the danger. *Fight or flight* is the common expression. (Prizefighters and runners are probably never nervous once their

*From *The Book of Lists, Number One*, by David Wallechinsky, Irving Wallace, and Amy Wallace. New York: Wm. Morrow, 1977.

events begin.) How can we respond to the fear induced by the "danger" of a presentation?

We cannot fight anyone; the audience is not the enemy. And even though all our instincts are telling us to flee, we must stand our ground. The result of our inability to respond to the danger shows up in all the destructive ways described earlier. The rapid breathing, the restless and aimless movements, the fiddling with objects, the vocal problems—all signs of nervousness—are the reactions of a body that wants to run but cannot. The discomfort and lack of naturalness are saying, "I want to be somewhere else."

What is this danger from which we cannot flee?

It turns out to be a many-headed monster. Working with hundreds of speakers has given me the opportunity to get a closer look at the monster's many unspeakably hideous faces. Here's a partial list of reasons why people dread speaking to a group:

- I have never given a speech before.
- I'm no good at public speaking.
- They may not like me.
- I may forget my material.
- I may make a fool of myself.
- I may fail.
- I may be embarrassed or humiliated.
- I have no control over the situation.
- I feel I'm being judged.
- They may be bored and ignore me.
- I may not have the answer to a question.
- People will discover my imperfections.
- I hate being the center of attention.
- I'm exposed.
- My credibility is at stake.
- I don't know what may go wrong.

On a less emotional level, a presentation is a kind of test—not simply a test of ideas, but a test of our ability to present and defend those ideas. As a rule, people do not like tests of any kind. But presentations are tests in which we are exposed; there is no place to hide. When you are standing alone in front of an audience it can be frightening. But a special kind of reward comes from knowing you can pass the test.

Subduing the Monster

So much for the negatives. What can be done to harness and control the forces of nervous energy? Plenty; let's divide the actions you can take into two categories: mental and physical preparation.

Mental Preparation It will not help much to belittle those fears listed above; they are real fears. Perhaps it may begin to help, however, by saying that those fears are nearly always unfounded. Each of us must look our monster in the eye and ask, "How terrible are you? What is the worst you can *actually* do to me? What is the likelihood that you are more myth than monster?"

Part of the solution lies in understanding audiences better as well as finding a better understanding of ourselves in the role of speaker.

Let's begin with the audience. They *want* you to succeed! Bear in mind that *you* are giving the presentation because you *know* things that the audience does not. Most of the time you know more than anyone else in the world about the specific details of your subject. It took time and effort to gain that knowledge, and that time and effort were part of the process that has prepared you to speak on your subject. The audience expects to receive something from you. They begin with the expectation that you know your subject. They will always give you the benefit of the doubt. In other words, you will have to *prove* your lack of knowledge. You begin the presentation with "money in the bank." Your job is to build on that capital by simply giving the audience what they expect.

Try to remember the worst presentation you ever saw. You very likely felt pity for the presenter. (Poor Fred . . . He's *dying* up there!) What made it a poor presentation was your disappointment in its lack of success. Not only do audiences expect you to succeed, they *want* you to succeed. The next time you give a presentation, look out at the faces and remember, *they are on your side.*

If you are concerned about not having control during a presentation, consider this. You are far less likely to be interrupted while you are speaking in a presentation than while speaking in a conversation. The presentation is a more formal method of communication than conversations or discussions. The unspoken rules don't encourage individual solo performances by audience members. And the bigger and more formal the presentation, the more unlikely it is that you will be interrupted at all. The entire process is designed to have the speaker in control.

Yes, it is possible to lose control momentarily. Yes, you will be interrupted from time to time, but nearly always because someone needs more information, doesn't understand a point, wishes to get your opinion on some facet of the subject, or wishes to contribute an example from his or her own experience. Yes, once in a blue moon someone will fire a seemingly hostile or a captious question. (Handling this situation will be covered a bit later.) But even this rare occurrence is but a brief lapse in your ongoing control of the communication process. In fact, the audience expects you to be in control.

Another thing to bear in mind about audiences: *They don't know how nervous you are.* While you are speaking, you may notice that your hand is a bit unsteady, but the audience won't be aware of it. Remember, their job is to listen to you, to look at the visuals, and to concentrate on your material. In order for them even to notice a sign of nervousness, that sign must be so obtrusive that it breaks through their concentration. And even if that does happen, it is only one of thousands of audio and visual pieces of information being processed by your audience.

One of the comments I often hear when presenters view themselves on video is, "Funny, when I gave that presentation I was really nervous, but it doesn't show up on the replay." It is interesting that when people become their *own* audience, *even they* cannot detect the signs of nervousness that seemed so obvious to them when they were making the presentation earlier.

Part of the problem is that you are trapped inside your own body. You know how your body normally feels. When you are nervous, it feels different in some ways. But you are the one who is in touch with what is going on in your body, *not* your audience. They don't know your mouth is dry. Don't blow little symptoms of nervousness all out of proportion. A little nervousness is a good thing; be prepared for it, but don't magnify it either in your eyes or those of your audience.

Let us turn the spotlight from the audience to you. What steps can you take to prepare yourself mentally to manage your nervous energy?

First, be ready for the flight-or-fight conflict. Decide before you go into the room you are *not* leaving until the presentation is over! You will stand your ground and grapple with the monster. You will use the presentation itself to release the pent-up energy.

Before the presentation, *visualize* your success. Find a quiet place where you can concentrate. Picture yourself speaking to your audience confidently and capably. See them in their seats concentrating on your material, looking at your visuals, nodding in agreement, taking notes, smiling. Vividly imagine as many details as you can. Visualization is curious stuff; it works only *if you think it does*. If you think it doesn't work, it doesn't (for you). You have probably heard more than one person say, "I can't see myself doing that!" That is exactly true. Before you can do something extraordinary, you must be able to "see" yourself doing it.

Examples of visualization are abundant in the world of sports, especially where great physical feats are required for victory. Watch the Olympic weight lifter staring off into space before making his attempt. He is concentrating on an image of himself raising that colossal weight over his head. The high jumper, preparing to hurl and snap his body over a bar well over seven feet off the ground, stands at the approach and, time after time, sees in his mind each step that will be taken, where the takeoff foot will be planted, and how his body will arch over, then fall on the other side of the bar. Listen to the words of Mark Gorsky, an American who won a gold medal in the 1984 Olympics, describing his mental rehearsal for the match sprint, a series of one-against-one bicycle races demanding enormous strength, endurance, will, and confidence:

> I had often imagined winning the gold medal. I had pictured every detail. I had seen every face in the crowd. I had rehearsed the strategy of each ride. And I have envisioned the incredible excitement and joy of Olympic victory.*

Try it; perhaps you are one of those for whom visualization works.

One of the best ways to control nervousness is through careful preparation of the presentation. The more thoughtfully and thoroughly you have prepared, the more confident you will be that you can handle anything that may happen. Careful preparation also frees you to concentrate more on your delivery.

For many people it is helpful to put the presentation into a more cosmic perspective. Ask yourself what lasting impact your presentation will have on the course of world history. Another approach is to ask what is the worst thing that can happen. This is trickier, because one can begin to imagine all sorts of nightmares. *Be realistic*—how often does an audience leap out of its chairs and attack the presenter? At how many presentations have you seen the audience throw objects at the speaker? It is one thing to try to anticipate difficult questions or even to plan for handling difficult people. It is quite another to dwell on imaginary and totally improbable disasters.

Far more useful is to shift your focus away from yourself and onto your audience. Remember, the whole purpose of the presentation is for you to give them something they need. What are those needs? How can you best satisfy them? What will some of *their* problems be in receiving and dealing with your material? How can you help them?

Another part of mental preparation is the awareness that the peak of nervousness always occurs at the beginning of a presentation. Once you get past the first two to five minutes, you will begin to return to reasonable normalcy. You will settle in to yourself, find that quiet center, and begin to be more relaxed. Expect to be nervous at the outset. Be confident that it will pass.

Physical Preparation Wear clothing that helps you to feel confident.

Before the presentation, try tensing your muscle systems then gradually releasing them. While you are in that quiet place you chose for your mental preparation, get comfortably seated. Begin with the muscles of your face.

*From *Bicycling* magazine, February 1988. Reprinted with permission.

Make them as tense as possible, then slowly release them until they are completely relaxed. Work downward through the rest of your muscle groups—neck, shoulders, arms, hands, stomach, legs, feet—get each muscle system as loose as possible. This process will help your body to remain relaxed. Get used to the feeling.

Do not use drugs to relax. Your presentation will suffer. You may *feel* you are giving a marvelous presentation, but you will be the only person in the room with that feeling. You need to be at the pinnacle of alertness and energy and at your sharpest focus to conduct a successful presentation. Drugs tend to dull your performance. Avoid coffee and cigarettes; they both stimulate the flow of adrenaline, heightening your nervousness.

Speaking to a group is demanding on the voice. Moreover, even mild nervousness tends to produce a dry throat. Make sure you have a pitcher of water and a glass handy before you begin.

Lastly, be sure that all your equipment and materials are in order.

During the Presentation   Choose a light, humorous beginning to help ease you through those first few minutes. This does not necessarily mean telling a joke, but a friendly, relaxed conversational exchange with your audience can convince you that they are not ready to commit mayhem upon your person. Communication is rooted in sharing. Begin by talking about something you possess, in common with your audience, if possible. This should help you and your audience get comfortable with each other and convince you that giving the presentation will not be so painful after all. If appropriate, use occasional light touches of humor to create a relaxed atmosphere.

Instead of thinking about speaking to "the audience," think about speaking to only one member of the audience at a time. After all, you can look at only one person at a time when establishing eye contact. Talking to a group of people is really an extension of talking to an individual—a skill we acquired as children.

Effective delivery requires normal breathing. If you detect breathing problems or frequent sighing, take a breathing break. Pause. Breath in slowly and deeply. Exhale slowly and deliberately. Don't hurry. Take a sip of water if you need to be doing something while taking your break.

While you are presenting, use your nervous energy constructively. Mobilize it. Move your hands and the rest of your body naturally. Move about the room—not in frenetic, perpetual, distracting motion, but in purposeful, even planned, ways. Get close to your audience. Use your eyes and your voice to contact everyone in the room. Focus the energy *outward,* not inward. Fill the room with your presence. Good delivery is *work*. The best thing to do with nervous energy is to put it to work.

If you draw a blank mentally, *do not freeze!* Your audience is not aware of your momentary lapse. Keep talking. It doesn't have to be about the specific point you are reaching for, just keep talking about your subject. Look for a handle—something you can grasp to work back into your material. Use the visual; you put it there to serve as a cue card. Have faith . . . two things will happen if you keep talking. First, you will find your way back to your script, and second, the audience will never know you lost your place.

If you feel your mouth getting a bit dry, pause. Take a sip of water. Give your audience a mini break. They can use a little change of pace, too.

Putting It in Perspective

Being nervous in front of an audience is commonplace. Everyone experiences it to some degree. It is not a sign of weakness, defective character, emotional deficiency, or lack of intelligence. It is *human*. Part of effective delivery depends on feeling good about yourself. Unless you have an unusual problem with self-image, you can develop a sense of confidence and well-being by simply practicing and enjoying a few successes.

We have examined a list of ways to prepare mentally and another list of physical preparations. Please review them when you give your next presentation. Beyond that, be aware that the single most effective way to learn to manage nervousness is *practice*. The secret you should know is that destructive nervous energy can be overcome by speaking to audiences several times. Each time you engage an audience, you get more used to the experience, your skills improve, and so does your self-assurance.

Practice with your presentation skills is available from an organization called Toastmasters International, a nonprofit, nonpartisan, nonsectarian educational organization of Toastmaster clubs throughout much of the world. The address is 2200 N. Grand Ave., Santa Ana, CA 92711. Although I have never joined, the positive experiences of others who have, and a careful review of the Toastmaster literature, have convinced me that much benefit can be derived from participation in their program. Practice can also be gained by enrolling in a public speaking course at your local college or university. Some colleges are even offering complete courses of study in business and technical presentations, rather than simply concentrating on speaking.

The war of nerves is one we all must fight, but one in which no one need become a casualty.

Five Guideposts to Effective Delivery

Here are the five ideas to bear in mind when delivering a presentation:

1. *Engagement*—Make human contact with your audience and build a relationship with its members.

2. *Energy*—Work at reaching your audience. Communicate an intensity and involvement in your subject.
3. *Empathy*—Focus on your audience and their needs, not on yourself. Become your audience.
4. *Keep Going*—Be prepared for mishaps and imperfections. Don't be overwhelmed by them. Don't magnify them by pointing them out, dwelling on them, or apologizing.
5. *Manage Your Nervous Energy*—Be aware it's normal. Prepare physically and mentally. Use the energy as a force to reach your audience and hold their attention.

Let's now move from general rules to specific pointers on how to deliver a presentation effectively.

EFFECTIVE DELIVERY TECHNIQUES

Next in importance to achieving the behavioral objective of your presentation is the immediate objective of getting your audience to listen and pay attention. The mere fact that the audience is in the room is no assurance that they will listen. The list of reasons why we don't listen is quite long. Here are just a few of those reasons:

* The room is uncomfortable or contains physical distractions.
* We decide we don't *want* to know anything about the topic.
* We are preoccupied with our always pressing personal agenda.
* We decide that we have nothing to gain by listening.
* The presentation is so poorly organized, it's hard to follow.
* We decide in advance that the speaker cannot impart anything worthwhile, either because we don't like that speaker for whatever reason, or we feel the speaker is deficient in some way.
* The level of detail is inappropriate for our needs—either too much or, worse, not enough.
* We don't understand the speaker's language.
* Poor delivery.

The last item can have the most devastating effect on your audience's ability (and willingness) to listen. On the other hand, *effective delivery can overcome every item on the list except extreme cases of the first item!*

The physical act of delivering a presentation requires that you use your voice and your body to communicate with your audience. Let us examine how engagement, energy, and empathy can influence the dynamics of speech and the attitudes and actions of the body to enhance that communication.

Style

Everyone has an individual speaking style. Your style is part of you. Your audience wants to get a sense of your style. Let's *not* begin by saying that only one ideal speaking style exists and we must all strive to achieve it. No, a multitude of speaking styles can be successful. If we all spoke exactly alike, it would be monotonous (and a little scary).

Within that framework of your basic speaking style is a range of choices for optimizing your delivery technique. You can, for example, insist that repeatedly staring at the floor while you think of your next utterance is part of your style. This section will attempt to convince you that floor staring is one facet of your style that needs to be changed. You can make that and many similar adjustments while still keeping your essential speaking style.

Let's begin.

The Voice

In an audiovisual presentation, the voice is the audio channel, carrying half the message. Thus, half the task of making contact with the audience depends on what you do with your vocal chords. What you do with your voice can mean the difference between an audience that is working to listen and one that is simply loafing. What are the characteristics that make a voice *listenable?*

Volume

Most beginning presenters speak too softly to audiences. Clearly you cannot conduct an effective presentation if no one can hear you. The usual solution is to advise people to speak up or project the voice to the back of the room. Good advice, but we should go beyond merely speaking louder.

We can divide our vocal and physical presence—the way we project the voice and body—into zones of communication. Our behavior changes as the zones change.

The smallest is the *intimate zone.* In the intimate zone, we bend close to each other and whisper. The intent is to contain the sounds and restrict them to the participants. Little or no body movement is used beyond, perhaps, cupping the hand over the listener's ear. In the *personal zone* (about four to six feet), we converse with little attempt to project the voice and we use small movements of the head, hands, and shoulders. In the *social zone* (six to 12 feet), we begin to project our voices outward and to use the body—especially the head, shoulders, and hands—to emphasize our words. Imagine a party with six or eight people standing in a circle. As the conversation shifts from person to person, each member of the group must project the voice to all others in the circle. In the *group zone* (12 to 40 feet or more), we are speaking to audiences. Here we must raise the volume of the voice to fill the room. This requires constant effort and may seem unnatural to those unaccustomed to speaking in the group zone. Such constant effort is, nonetheless, utterly necessary. Moreover, the body movements in this zone are markedly more pronounced than in other zones *for natural or for practiced speakers.*

Experienced speakers develop a sense of the size of the acoustic space they are in and fill that space with their voices. Acoustic space does not refer simply to the size of the room. Many other factors affect how well the voice will carry. Certain acoustic characteristics of the environment tend to absorb the voice and thus expand the acoustic space. Among these are the number of people in the room, drapes on the walls, thick rugs on the floor, and absorbent acoustic tile on the ceiling. Notice that accomplished speakers tailor their body movements to the space—the larger the space, the more pronounced the movement. The levels of volume and presence that are correct for a group of 15 in a small room are not at all correct for a group of 50 in a large hall. Inexperienced speakers are likely to use the same volume level for both spaces.

Another problem to avoid is "trailing off." The volume level is fine until the speaker approaches the end of the sentence. In thinking about what to say next, the speaker gives up on volume. The audience has to deal with a succession of incomplete utterances. If you have this tendency, you must train yourself to "keep your foot on the gas" until you complete your sentences.

A final bit of advice: If you must err with your volume level, let it be on the side of too much volume, not too little. (Remember Rule Number Two: Energy.) If you feel you are speaking a bit too loudly, chances are it's perfect.

Vocal Pace

Have you ever listened to a speaker who spoke too fast or too slowly? If so, you may recall how frustrating it was that you could not control the pace. You may also recall how easy it was to focus your eyes on the middle distance and slip away mentally. Now change roles. You are the speaker. You control the vocal pace. It is up to you to choose the rate at which your audience will hear your words. How do you choose? It's not a simple matter. Here are some guidelines to help you decide at what pace to speak.

Do Not Rush   An audience can process words for short periods at better than 800 words per minute, but you cannot possibly talk that fast and shouldn't try. Nonetheless, one of the most common errors made by unskilled speakers is talking too fast, probably induced by nervousness. A too-rapid delivery strips the voice of all the elements of listenability for the sake of speed. The voice tends to become flat and mechanical. Pauses are rare. The faster the pace, the more difficult it becomes to speak distinctly. We begin to stumble over our words. The audience (despite its capacity to process 800 plus words per minute) soon grows tired of the sheer work required. The flat voice, stumbling over words, lack of pauses, and strenuous effort required to keep listening together cause all but the most heroic audience members to drop out. The ideal pace is quick enough to hold the audience's attention without impairing listenability and inducing fatigue.

Do Not Dawdle   If the vocal pace is too slow, the audience will have too much free time. Audience members will always use the extra time to think about subjects unrelated to yours but of immediate and compelling interest to them. Eventually, those preoccupations begin to command most of their attention. Sooner or later members return from their ruminations (or their reveries) to your words only to discover they missed something important. Then, faced with the double problem of not understanding a speaker whose delivery is ponderously slow, they return permanently to their private worlds of thought . . . and your voice . . . fades . . . into oblivion. . . .

Vary the Pace   Wouldn't it be convenient if some expert discovered that the ideal vocal pace is exactly 148 words per minute? We could practice with a tape recorder until we spoke automatically at the perfect rate. We would never have to be concerned about pace again. Unfortunately, there is no single ideal pace. An audience is composed of people who react individually to your voice. An ideal pace for one person may seem a bit fast or slow for someone in the next seat. Speaking at one pace would also be boring. Try to imagine how difficult it would be to listen to someone speaking at the same unvarying rate for an hour. Audiences expect changes of pace; it's part of what makes vocal delivery interesting.

Just as important is the relationship between *idea density* and vocal pace. Idea density refers to the complexity of your material and the speed at which the audience must process it mentally. It makes sense to speak more slowly when explaining complex material or stressing a key point or conclusion. It is equally sensible to quicken the pace when covering material the audience can easily absorb. In fact, not to do so runs the risk of losing out to our old enemy, preoccupation.

Use Feedback   Look and listen for the messages from your audience. Confused expressions, gestures of helplessness, blank stares, head held in the hands, or heads shaking "no" usually mean that you are speaking too fast (or that the idea density is too difficult for them to cope with). These signals could also mean that it's time to stop and test what people have on their minds. They may need help. Slouching or languid posture, staring at the floor, doodling, and vacant expressions are signals that you should pick up the pace. The ideal pace is constantly varying to suit *this* audience, *this* information, and the needs of *this* moment in the presentation.

Pauses

Closely related to vocal pace is the subject of how to use pauses in delivery. Most beginning speakers fail to pause at all (beyond the unavoidable stops to inhale). This is usually due to nervousness and a lack of empathy—to an inward rather than an outward focus. Accomplished speakers, in contrast, use pauses deliberately and effectively. Pauses not only make the voice more listenable, they have useful roles to play in delivery. The three types of pause are:

1. *Rest*—These pauses provide relief. After a fashion, people get used to your voice. Part of what makes music listenable are the *rests*—the silences that heighten the complexity and enrich the overall beauty of the sound patterns. Listening, as you know, is hard work. An occasional pause merely for a brief relaxation from our labors is a welcome change.

2. *Reinforcement*—This pause comes *after* you have made a telling point, explained a key relationship, or reached an important conclusion or milestone. The pause reinforces the point. First, your pause by itself indicates that the point is important. Second, the pause gives the audience time to let the point register.

3. *Anticipation*—The speaker builds to a climactic point then pauses, holding the audience in suspense, before delivering the climax.

> Example: "I realize that if we approve this ordinance, only one person in 900,000 will contract cancer. Most citizens would agree that it's an acceptable risk. But do you know who that one cancer victim is? That person is . . . [pause and slowly look at everyone in the room] . . . that person is one of *you!*" (A bit melodramatic, but you see the point.)

It is easy to misuse pauses. For example, constantly stopping in the middle of thoughts creates a disjointed effect that audiences find distracting. We normally speak in sentences. Avoid pausing in the middle of sentences and racing past the "periods." Combining misplaced pauses with excessively fast delivery leads to an annoying "machine-gun" effect. In fact, *any* repetitive pattern will eventually become annoying. Too many pauses will create the impression that you are constantly collecting your thoughts. Very long pauses at inappropriate places make you seem lost.

Pauses are essential to listenability. Without them, the voice becomes uninteresting. Beginners tend to avoid pausing in part because they are overly sensitive to silences. The silence seems much longer (and hence more awkward) to the inexperienced speaker than it does to the audience. If the patterns of sounds and *silences* make music interesting, such patterns are even more vital in speeches, where the patterns carry information.

Animation

The word comes from the Latin *animare:* to quicken, enliven, or endow with breath or soul. When applied to speech, animation is the quality that enlivens the voice—that gives it vitality and interest. The animation in your voice tells the audience how you feel about your words. Take any simple word, such as "yes." If you were simply to say the word with no frame of reference, your voice would lack animation. Now say "yes" in response to the following questions:

Is this your wallet, mister?
Haven't I warned you a thousand times this would happen?
Don't you think it's high time you gave him a piece of your mind?
Do you really love me, Harold?

The differences you hear in your voice are differences in *animation.* Animation is composed of many elements, such as pitch (intonation and inflection) and stress (volume changes). Animation tells the audience we are alive. It also contributes to the meaning of our statements:

"Willard, the way you drive this car is *incredible!*" How you say that last word has a lot to do with what we learn about Willard's driving skills.

Without animation, the voice becomes lifeless and uninteresting. In films—especially the older ones—robots are almost always given flat, mechanical voices. Being lifeless creatures, they are expected to sound lifeless. A human voice without animation is described as a monotone and is just as deadening. Few things short of knock-out drops can induce sleep more quickly than a monotone.

Of course, it is possible to carry animation to extremes. Occasionally (but rarely) a speaker's animation is so exaggerated and bubbly that it seems contrived and unnatural. By far the more common problem, however, is little or no animation at all.

Two other problems related to animation are *ending declarative statements with upward inflections* and *"sing-song" delivery.*

One of the conventions of our language is that of ending questions with an upward inflection and declarative statements with a downward inflection:

Are we going to the meeting? (Do you hear the upward inflection in the word "meeting"?)
We are going to the meeting. (Now listen to the downward inflection at the end.)

Some speakers have the habit of ending *declarative* statements with *upward* inflections. This gives their statements a tentative, questioning, uncertain, even pleading quality. The solution is to develop the habit of ending declarative statements with positive, forceful downward inflections.

"Sing-song" delivery is repeating the same inflection pattern so frequently that it becomes distracting or tedious. The problem is most pronounced when the speaker is providing a list of items to the audience. Usually the last syllable of each item on the list gets an upward inflection, but not always. It's the repetition of the pattern that makes it distracting, not the pattern itself. Use a variety of inflections, especially when listing items.

Your voice should carry your convictions, concerns, and feelings by the way you stress certain syllables and the way you change your voice's intonation and inflections.

Vocal Noise

Vocal noise is the verbal litter that clutters our speech. Some of the most common examples of these non-words are *ah, you know (y'know), I mean, like, um, ok (also k), now, right, he goes, and.* It is possible to utter entire sentences consisting of only vocal noise:

"You know, I mean like you know what I mean, right?"

Vocal noise is distracting. If you use *any* expression frequently enough, your audience will become aware of it. For example, an associate manages to work the term "certainly" into almost every sentence. The unfortunate problem with vocal noise is not just that it is inelegant, sloppy speech, but that eventually the audience will concentrate on the noise and not the message.

Vocal noise is our way of filling the gaps in speech. The brain needs time to encode the next message. While the brain is working to turn thoughts into words, the vocal chords are stalling for time. We keep our vocal motor running to let our listeners know that the next message is on the way, to keep from being interrupted, and to fill the time with speech, even if it is sterile, useless speech.

Vocal noise can be eradicated through a two-step process. First, you must *become aware* that your speech contains the noise. This is not as simple as it may seem. Those who have the problem never hear the noise; they are concentrating on the real words:

(I mean) if you listen to (you know) your own voice, (like) eventually you (ah) will (you know) begin to (like) hear the garbage.

Admittedly, this example is a caricature, but it is hard to imagine that a person whose expression contained that much ugly excess baggage wouldn't want to purge it. Unfortunately, we just don't hear it in our own speech. The first step involves critical self-hearing. At your next presentation, have your voice audiotaped, then review the tape carefully. You cannot stop making the noise until you can detect it. An occasional "um" or "you know" is not a serious problem. If you do detect an annoying frequency of noise, you must be prepared to hear it as you actually speak.

Step two: Be confident and comfortable enough to let silences occur where you now use noise. Vocal noise is the enemy of the pause, and in this struggle, you must be on the side of the pause.

Articulation and Pronunciation

Audiences can react unfavorably to the way you speak your words. Have you ever heard these "words"?

gonna, coulda, wooda, din't, effit, tenative, twenny, deeze

Yes, we hear them all the time. We scarcely notice any but the most flagrant cases of sloppy speech *in conversations.*

But we *do* notice poor enunciation in a speaker. The rules change. Not that audiences expect perfection; they don't. In fact, if you were to articulate every sound with utter perfection, your voice would sound artificial, contrived, and unnatural and that too would become a distraction. Unfortunately, we do tend to judge a speaker's intelligence or competence (almost always incorrectly) if we hear many words spoken sloppily or incorrectly. It is, therefore, a good idea to speak distinctly and pronounce your words correctly when talking to an audience (or anyone, for that matter), not merely to avoid sending false messages about your intelligence but also to ensure that your words are easily understood.

Nervousness often causes us to speak too quickly. The more quickly we speak, the more difficult it becomes to articulate our words. Frequently the simple advice, "Slow down and speak more carefully" works wonders with a nervous speaker. A more serious problem occurs when we have built-in articulation or pronunciation difficulties; that is, when we say certain words carelessly or incorrectly under any circumstances.

The first step in correcting ingrained articulation problems is the same as that for correcting vocal noise, you must *hear yourself.* Once you recognize the little flaws in your speech, you can work to eliminate them. Use a tape recorder, as before. Read a long passage (at least five minutes) to ensure that you have dropped your tape recorder voice. The passage should be written in conversational language to simulate normal speech. An even better method is to record your voice in a real speech. When you play the tape, listen carefully to how you articulate your words. Listen for missing *t*'s, *d*'s, *ing*'s, or the substituting of a single sound for a whole word, such as *shoulda* for *should have.*

Listen for missing sounds. You need to listen to your voice with critical ears, otherwise the careless enunciation will go unnoticed. Would you pass *goverment,* for example? How about *intresting, seprit, persnell,* or *confrence?* Don't ignore even tiny words. The word *the* can become a clipped attachment to a word beginning with a vowel, as in *thestimate* or *thoffice.*

Listenforatendencytojamwordstogether. Listen for a distinct separation between words.

Listen to the pronunciation of the words. Some words are mispronounced by almost anyone; such words include *nuclear, junta, irrevocable, clandestine,* and *inexplicable.* Only the most discriminating and critical audience member will be distracted by these and similar words. But simple words are another story. Listen for *an* instead of *and, uv* instead of *of, fer* instead of *for,* and *ta* instead of *to.*

The second step in correcting poor articulation is systematically to remove your careless speech habits. Fill in the missing sounds, separate your words, use the correct pronunciations. Listen again and again; keep practicing. In short, work at speaking carefully. The goal is to communicate with your audience without diverting its attention or conveying the wrong impression about you because of careless speech habits.

To heighten your sensitivity to this subject, here are several examples of articulation and pronunciation problems:

Omitting Part of the Word

antartic for antarCtic	joolry for jEWELry
asterik for asteriSk	labratory for labOratory
auxillary for auxilIary	persnell for persOnnel
Barbra for BarbAra	praps for pErHaps
boundry for boundAry	probly for probABly
comftable for comfORtable	repetoir for repeRtoire
choklit for chocOlate	sussinct for suKsinkt
diffrent for diffERent	spose for sUppose
dimond for diAmond	suprise for suRprise
din't for diDn't	tenative for tenTative
Febuary for FebRuary	twenny for twenTy
govament for govERNment	ushuly for usUally
hierachial for hierarchiCal	vegtables for vegEtables
intresting for intEResting	vunerable for vuLnerable

Dropping Word Endings

crep (for crept), doin', goin', talkin', walkin', etc.

Adding Sounds

athAlete for athlete

ideaR for idea

poTpouree for pohpouree

misschEEveeus for MISSchivus

Producing the Wrong Sounds

The Word(s)	Is Pronounced	Not
accept	aksept	asept
err	ur (or) er	air
escape	escape	excape
et cetera	et settera	ek settera
memento	memento	momento
nuclear	nyooklear	newkular or newkeeah
peripheral	periferal	perifeeal
picture	piktcher	pitcher or pitcha
primer	primr	prymer (set of basic instructions)
remunerate	remyoonerate	renumerate
rapport	rahpour	reepour or reeport
Saturday	Saturday	Saterdee
sinecure	synekure or sinekure	syneshure
subsidiary	subsidee ery	subsider ery
to	to	ta
window	window	windah

Stress on the Wrong Syllable

Correct	Incorrect or Not Preferred
akYOOmen	AKumen
FORMidable	forMIDable
IMPetent	imPOTent
irREParable	irrePAIRable
LAMentable	laMENTable
teLEPathy	TELapathy

Sloppy Speech

ahdunno for I don't know

gonna for going to

oughta for ought to

wanna for want to

whaddya for what do you

whadja for what did you

and my favorite . . . jeet jet for did you eat yet?

If You Have an Accent

Many speakers who have accents or pronounced dialects are unnecessarily concerned about them. In working with many hundreds of speakers, I have encountered just one whose accent prevented the audience from understanding parts of the speech. In this one case, the speaker had been in this country just three months and was still learning English. Usually it takes two or three minutes for the audience to become familiar with an accent. After that, they largely ignore it and concentrate on the ideas being conveyed.

If you have an accent, remember to speak a bit more slowly than you normally do in conversations. It is important that the entire audience understand you. It may take a little time before everyone becomes familiar with your accent, so speak very slowly for the first two minutes or so. Lastly, *never apologize for an accent or feel self-conscious about it.* Most people genuinely enjoy the special flavor of an accent or dialect, especially if the speaker pronounces the words carefully.

Variety

Volume, vocal pace, animation, and pauses are all key elements in effective vocal delivery, but *variety* is the indispensable ingredient in a listenable voice. Variety means changing the pace to suit the audience's needs: a slower delivery when the material is difficult or when every word must be stressed to hammer home a point, faster when the ideas are simple or you wish to convey the impression of haste or speed in your material. Variety also means changing the volume, not necessarily from a roar to a whisper—that's a bit too theatrical—but within reasonable limits, for changes in volume add interest and excitement to your vocal delivery. Notice, incidentally, how the most experienced speakers often make their most telling points in the quietest voice.

They also vary the animation level as they speak. Experienced speakers, who speak with considerable animation, often use a monotone to make important points, because of the striking contrast. Changes in animation are not only desirable, but in a long presentation they are essential. We are all aware that a monotone eventually causes audience members to drift either into their private worlds or into slumber. The same can be true of a continuously highly animated (or bubbly) voice. In fact, even if your speaking voice has good animation, if you speak for more than 20 minutes or so, your audience gets used to how you sound. They become accustomed to the same pause patterns, volume level, pitch, and pace. Experienced speakers realize that the key to a listenable voice is change—changes in pitch, inflection, and stress. They also realize the impact of using occasional, short periods of flat, unanimated delivery to make a point by contrasting with the otherwise highly animated, emphatic peaks in their presentations.

Variety is usually one of the last vocal characteristics we acquire as speakers, perhaps because it requires some practice and a bit of courage. It is far safer to have a laid back, "businesslike" voice. Variety, nonetheless, is the one crucial element in vocal delivery that separates the competent from the accomplished.

The Body

An effective speaker engages an audience not just with the voice. Making contact also requires the use of the entire body. Some parts of our anatomies are more important than others. That makes sense. After all, how much more important is the knee cap as opposed to the eyes for making contact?

The Eyes

The most important feature you have for making contact with your audience is your eyes. When you are speaking to an audience, you should be spending *all* of your time looking at their eyes. True, 100 percent eye contact is not possible. Occasionally, to pick up your next cue, it is necessary to glance at an overhead transparency or the visual being projected on the screen. These breaks in eye contact should account for no more than about 5 percent of the total.

Eye contact works the same way in presentations as it does in conversations. It signals the listener that you are concerned that he or she is getting the message and responding to it. Eye contact tells audience members that you are looking for feedback, that *they* can communicate with *you,* even if their nonverbal message is simply, "I'm listening." In some cultures, prolonged eye contact is a sign of disrespect or challenge. In western culture, it is generally a sign of truthfulness, of respect, and of being attentive. Eye contact says nonverbally, "I want to communicate with you."

Audience members can easily feel ignored, uninvolved, and neglected when they do not receive eye contact from a speaker. Similarly, an experienced speaker becomes concerned when someone in the audience constantly avoids eye contact or shifts the eyes in avoidance. Notice the behavior of people in a serious argument. If differences become drastic enough, they begin to avoid eye contact. This is especially true of the person in the listening mode. The tendency is to look away—either downward or often up at the ceiling with an expression of suffering or impatience. The nonverbal message is clear: "Your words are not reaching me."

Important as it is, eye contact seems to be ignored by many speakers, especially beginners. They seem hypnotized by the floor, or by shoes, wallpaper, lighting fixtures, or by the most powerful eye magnet of all, *the screen.* It is not uncommon to see entire presentations being delivered to the screen!

Some speakers have the habit of staring pensively into space, waiting for their next thought to take shape.

Occasionally a speaker with these difficulties claims, "I can't think when I'm looking at someone else; it distracts me." Yet the same person has no difficulty whatsoever in maintaining eye contact during a conversation. We learned to communicate that way as children; it comes naturally to us. Usually what distracts these speakers is the sheer number of people with whom eye contact is to be made. The secret is to apply to larger groups the same easy, natural eye contact we use in conversations with one or two people. It's not really difficult. Here are a few tips:

Look at Everyone Some speakers confine their eye contact to those in the center or on one side of the room. It takes extra effort to reach the extreme edges of your audience. By all means make the effort. Never exclude anyone from eye contact. Develop an awareness of how much time you are spending just sending and receiving messages through people's eyes. Develop an awareness of whom you are looking at and for how long. Everyone in the room should get roughly the same amount of eye contact. Never give any one person excessive amounts of eye contact. This is especially likely to happen when one person in the audience greatly outranks everyone else. When the high ranking person gets most of the eye contact, it makes him or her uncomfortable and it annoys everyone else, because they feel they are being ignored.

Occasionally you may notice someone in your audience who is sending great gobs of approving signals back to you—smiling, nodding in agreement as you make your points, reacting favorably to everything you say. Congratulations, but be careful of a trap. The inexperienced speaker, having discovered at least one friendly face, will repeatedly come back for more reassurance. The one "fan" will get most of the eye contact, and you will annoy everyone else.

Take Your Time It takes time to establish eye contact. Look at each audience member for at least three to five seconds. Flitting from face to face is not making eye contact. It is merely going through the motions, and your audience will know it. It takes time for the messages to go out from you: "Are you with me?" . . . "Do you agree?" . . . "Does this give you a problem?" . . . "Do you understand?" And then more time must elapse to get the nonverbal answers back.

Don't Be Trapped The projection screen can have a magnetic attraction for the eyes, and so can overhead transparencies or a demonstration model. Be aware of how much time you are taking away from your audience by staring hypnotically and needlessly at any object in the room. An alarm bell should go off in your head.

Avoid Mechanical Eye Contact   Eye contact should be *random* and natural. Avoid having your face look like a radar dish, scanning the audience as if it were a squadron of aircraft.

"Read" Your Audience   Look for facial expressions, posture, movement, and gestures. Audience members will usually tell you when they agree or disagree, understand or are confused, are keeping up or flagging in their interest, are comfortable or uncomfortable. Be sensitive to these unspoken messages and be ready to react to them by changing your pace, stopping to ask for questions, or taking a break. Eye contact benefits the speaker as well as the audience.

The Hands

Even though we need our hands for an endless variety of useful things (such as eating, dressing, driving), when most of us are before an audience, our hands become an embarrassment. They loom larger than life. We look for places to hide them—in our armpits, behind our backs, in our pockets. Yet the hands can speak an eloquent language of their own if we let them.

The first rule of the hands is that they appear natural. The minimum requirement is that the hands do not become a distraction on which the audience can focus its attention. Playing with pointers, fiddling with pens or pencils, fingering cue cards, scratching repeatedly, fussing with glasses—these and countless similar nervous and pointless uses of the hands only detract from the presentation.

Once we prevent the hands from becoming a distraction, we enter the neutral state where they neither help nor hinder delivery. The hands hang from the sides, or one hand is in a pocket while the other either rests on a table or lectern, holds notes, or is simply held in front of the body. In this neutral state, the key is that the hands appear *natural*. They neither add to nor distract from the delivery style.

With more accomplished—and more dynamic—presenters, the hands *add* their own dimension. The hands move to stress or underscore the words, bringing their own expressive dynamics to the delivery. We are, of course, discussing gestures. The roundabout way used to sneak up on the word *gestures* is necessary because the word's reputation is somewhat tarnished in some quarters. One imagines the high school teacher admonishing the dull-witted student, "You have to use more gestures, Arnold!" No expert in oral communication claims that gestures are mandatory. But neither are seasonings in food.

The problem with the dictum "use gestures" is that many people are uncomfortable *showing* their hands, let alone moving them expressively. Sadly, the audience shares this discomfort immediately and profoundly. The movements (for the sake of "using gestures") appear wooden, contrived, and inappropriate. It is far better to be yourself—to appear natural—than to make gestures. The curious fact, however, is that *nearly everyone uses gestures when they speak in everyday conversation.* It is natural to do so. (Observe your friends at the next social event you attend.) In a presentation the feeling of being "on stage" inhibits us from letting our hands behave normally.

Many speakers deliver their entire presentations with hands jutting stiffly at their sides, or rubbing them together (to generate heat, presumably), or toying with some object, or in an attitude of prayer, or wringing each other in a contest for domination, or clutching a lectern in white-knuckle desperation. Then after the planned part of the presentation ends, as the speaker begins to respond to questions, the hands suddenly become natural and expressive. The reason, of course, is that when answering questions, we are no longer presenting, but merely responding to one other person as we would in a conversation.

Here are a few thoughts to help you with your hands, the third most expressive part of your body (after your voice and your eyes).

Be Natural As a minimum goal, your hands should not distract the audience. Don't play with objects or do awkward things with your hands.

Hold Your Hands in Front of You It is best to carry your hands between your waist and shoulders. Try simply placing one hand in the other when you begin. As you warm up, eventually you will begin to move your hands.

Do Not "Make" Gestures Gestures occur naturally. Never force them; simply allow them to happen. Gestures help you to dissipate nervous energy in ways that enhance communication. They need not be meaningful or pictorial in order to do so. Studied gestures look that way—studied, forced.

Do Not Use the Same Gesture Repeatedly Constant karate chops, hammer blows, finger thrusts, and the like are as distracting as wooden gestures.

Gestures Should Be Appropriate Huge, sweeping, or theatrical gestures are out of place in a business presentation; they are much more suited to a football rally or the stage. Use gestures to punctuate and stress, to accompany your words, not to dominate visually.

Don't Overdo Gestures Ever see a speaker who has a gesture for nearly every word? Being a gesture machine can be the pinnacle of distraction. Use gestures only for emphasis; otherwise their effect is lost.

Open the Circle   Hold your arms out straight to the side. Think of your hands, arms, and shoulders as a line. By clasping your hands, the line becomes a circle. You also form a circle when you clutch an object, such as a pen, or pointer, or lectern with both hands, or put both hands in your pockets. The hands become grounded, incapable of gestures. Try to keep the circle open as much as possible—open to let the audience in, not closed to keep them out.

Experts in nonverbal communication point out that showing the palms of the hands is a sign of openness, honesty, and friendliness. Apparently the symbolism goes back to the Stone Age, when not having a rock in your hand was a good way to make friends. When soldiers surrender, the characteristic gesture is to raise the arms and show the palms of the hands. When one raises one's right hand to swear an oath, the palm always faces outward. Just as making a fist can communicate negatively in most situations, so can showing the palms create a positive reaction.

So much for the hands. What about the rest of the body?

Posture

We communicate information through the ways we hold, move, and array our bodies. How should you present your body? Once again, the goal is to be natural—to be yourself. Posture and attitude are often problems for inexperienced speakers. Figure 22 illustrates four positions commonly used by inexperienced speakers, all of which are to be avoided.

Positions A and B are from the military. They are designed to hold the body rigid and motionless. Position A is attention and B is parade rest. They

| A | B | C | D |

Figure 22   Four Positions to Avoid

both seem stiff and unnatural to an audience. Both communicate a sense that the speaker is ill-at-ease. Position C is the police-chief posture. It seems to signal a kind of threatening authority and, at the same time, a bit of defensiveness or self-protection. Position C solves the problem of what to do with the embarrassing hands. They are inelegantly stuffed into the armpits. Position D is the most defensive of all. I call it the genital protective position, for obvious reasons. Position D is to be avoided for two reasons: First, it immobilizes the hands (closing the circle); second, it focuses attention on a part of your anatomy that you would prefer the audience would ignore!

All of these beginner positions are popular because they solve the problem of what to do with the hands. Each is awkward and tells the audience that you are probably uncomfortable. Other attitudes to avoid include slouching, draping the body over objects, standing with legs crossed or with most of the weight on one leg with one hip swung out to the side, leaning forward severely at the waist, holding hands on hips, or hooking thumbs into one's waistband.

What is left? Stand reasonably erect, with shoulders back (but not stiffly), head level and appearing natural and comfortable. Avoid a very wide stance; it makes you look awkward. Stand with your feet about as wide apart as your shoulders. That is how you look in a normal conversation. It works beautifully for a presentation, too.

The way you present your body—how you stand and move—influences your credibility and persuasiveness with your audience.

Movement

When you speak to an audience, motion is inevitable. Even the most rigid stance requires breathing and movements of the jaw and mouth. But how much movement is desirable? Part of what the audience sees is you. You become part of the visual information channel. You, in effect, become part of the message they receive. The simple needs for variety and interest require that you change position and even location where possible. When the space in which you are presenting allows it, move across the front of your audience. Get close to those in the front seats.

Do a little planning. Analyze the speaker's space and the audience's space. Where are the best places for you to stand? How can you move to those places naturally and unobtrusively? What spaces should you avoid moving into (such as in the path of the projector beam, or too close to an audience member, or in a place where you will be blocking the view of the screen for one or more audience members)? Remember to avoid moving in such a way that your back is turned to any member of your audience for more than a few seconds. Don't pace or stomp about the room. If you are changing overhead transparencies, don't wander too far from the projector.

The three keys to motion are to *avoid distractions, use motion expressively,* and *get close to your audience.*

Avoid Distractions

Any constantly repeated movement is likely to become a distraction. Swaying back and forth or from side to side, pacing, rocking, doing a little dance step, or using the same gesture endlessly are all distractions. Audiences are highly prone to being distracted. Don't give them the opportunity. Other examples of distracting movements include the following, *when done constantly:*

- Removing and replacing or adjusting eyeglasses
- Putting hands in and out of pockets
- Touching a part of the clothing
- Scratching or rubbing the same spot
- Playing with objects
- Running a hand through one's hair
- Readjusting a wayward lock of hair
- Adjusting the microphone
- Pointing to everything on the visual
- Fiddling with jewelry (ring twisting is a favorite)

Some movements need not be repeated to be distracting; they are intrusive the first time they are done. Examples of such motions are: jingling change in the pockets, banging the screen with a pointer, and/or fussing with an overhead transparency—once the visual is on the projector and looks reasonably framed on the screen, do not go back to readjust it. The whole screen will be filled with sudden, jerky movements while your audience is trying to read the visual.

Distractions—the enemies of presentations—come in three varieties:

1. *Preoccupation*—Every audience member has a personal collection of plans, problems, and concerns that is instantly available to compete with the presentation for attention.
2. *Environmental*—Physical distractions in the room can make concentrating on your presentation mildly difficult to nearly impossible. These environmental distractions were covered in Chapter 7.
3. *Delivery*—The third variety includes not just the distracting movements listed above, but *anything* the speaker does with the voice or body to divert the attention of the audience from the content of the presentation.

As the presenter, you cannot change the existence of the first variety of distractions, but by eliminating distractions in the environment and in delivery, you *can* hold the attention of your audience and reduce the likelihood that they will slip away mentally.

Use Motion Expressively

The earlier discussions of gestures may have left you with the impression that they are the exclusive property of the hands and arms. Not so. We use the head, shoulders, torso—standing on tiptoe is a gesture. President Franklin D. Roosevelt, who was paralyzed below the waist, had a powerful delivery style. He used his upper body to heighten and emphasize his points. The magnificent way he tossed his head was a gesture that he could have patented!

When you speak before an audience, your constant companion is a heightened level of nervous energy. The tendency to vent that energy through body motion is hard to suppress. The best course is *not* to suppress the energy. Use it to move naturally and forcefully to persuade your audience and build credibility.

Avoid nervous movements. The most obvious example is perpetual motion. Never move continuously. Stop frequently in places that will not obscure anyone's view of the screen. The vocal principles of the pause apply as well to body motion.

Get Close to Your Audience

Move as close to your audience as circumstances will permit. With a little practice, you will develop a sense of just how close you can get to people in the front row without encroaching on their personal space (about five or six feet). Do not stand in front of one person for long periods. Move naturally to another site in front of your audience.

If your audience is seated in a U-shaped arrangement, do not make the mistake of walking deeply into the U to get close. This forces your audience to look at an unchanging view of your back (not your best side).

Frequently, you will *not* have the freedom of movement to get as close to your audience as you wish. If you use an overhead projector, for example, you must remain close enough to change visuals. The worst case is when you must deliver a presentation while seated. Rather than speak while seated, try to arrange the seats and the screen so that you can move about with at least a few feet of leeway.

APPEARANCE

Earlier we emphasized that *you* are part of the presentation—part of the visual information gained by your audience. Most of what the audience sees of you—at least in area—is what you are wearing; thus, clothing is not a trivial subject. Your appearance is a commentary on the occasion. Your clothing, grooming, and jewelry, if any, form a nonverbal message on how important you think the presentation is. This notion is not old fashioned, either. People still dress up when they get married or attend functions they deem important. They dress for the occasion. Do not overinterpret this statement. You do not need to don a tuxedo or evening gown to deliver a presentation, but if your appearance is shabby or too casual, you may communicate an unintended message—that the presentation is not important to you, or that you are socially inept.

Our appearance also denotes the economic, professional, and social groups with which we identify. It's a statement on how we wish to be viewed by others. It is always a good idea to emphasize the similarities and downplay the differences between you and your audience. This applies in a limited way to your appearance. When you speak to business groups, wear business clothes. That does not mean wearing "the uniform," but it does mean avoiding casual clothes. If the occasion is less formal, dress informally but just as carefully. Aim for the high end of informal dress, not the opposite.

The wider variety of clothing that women choose from can pose problems of delivery. If the outfit is especially form-fitting or revealing, a woman speaker can introduce distractions by her mere presence, thus diverting attention from the message she is there to convey. This does not mean, incidentally, that a woman must dress plainly. It is easy to look feminine and attractive and at the same time professional, for want of a better word. One acquaintance tells me that she always takes the most direct approach by wearing an attractive three-piece business suit on the day of the presentation. She is convinced it has the added benefit of boosting her confidence. Men who share her feelings also wear their best business attire on such occasions.

One final pointer: Occasionally jewelry can be distracting. Audiences tend to notice when jewelry makes sounds or when it is especially striking.

A speaker's appearance is important. Give it some thought.

HOW TO USE VISUALS AND AUDIOVISUAL EQUIPMENT

Using Visuals

An important part of a polished delivery is skillfully controlling the visual channel. Using visuals smoothly and unobtrusively is not difficult. Like so many other facets of presentation skills, it requires an awareness and mastery of an accumulation of small details. Here are those details.

In General

Your most urgent concern should be that every member of your audience can see the visuals. Place the screen, easel, or chalkboard where it affords the best view. Arrange the chairs so that no one's view of the screen will be obscured. See Chapter 7 for more details. During the presentation, stand (or sit if you have to) where you will not block anyone's view.

The audience should never be conscious of the equipment or its use. Check out all the equipment in advance.

Avoid using notes. Your cues should all be on the visuals.

Face the audience. Look at the screen or the overhead transparency to pick up your cues. Visuals have the power to draw the eyes of some speakers and fix them hypnotically on the screen. Don't be trapped; use your eyes for making contact with your audience.

Use a pointer—not your finger—to point at the screen. The pointer is designed to do two things: (1) to focus your audience's attention on a part of the visual, and (2) to keep your body from blocking anyone's view while you are doing (1). Hold the pointer in the hand closer to the screen. Holding it in the other hand forces you to turn awkwardly into the screen. Don't point at everything on the visual; point out the highlights only. Don't bang the pointer on the screen or the chart. *Put it down when you are not using it,* and (for the last time) do not play with it. Telescoping pointers are enormously tempting. The urge to collapse and expand them is almost irresistible!

In presentations using overhead transparencies, you don't need a long pointer. Simply lay a pencil directly on the transparency with the point at the place you wish to highlight. A little nervous shaking of the hand looks like an advanced case of palsy on the screen, so don't try to hold the pointer.

When you want the audience to focus on you exclusively, snap off the overhead transparency projector. With 35mm, use a slide with a single bright color for the same purpose. White is too glaring. Black is unacceptable because the audience can't see you. Don't project visuals before you need them, and don't project them after you have finished with them.

If you must show the same visual twice, make two visuals. Do not waste time fumbling and searching for visuals that have to perform double duty. Making extra copies of overhead transparencies or 35mm slides is easy and inexpensive.

Practice using the equipment. Fortunately, most audiovisual equipment is easy to operate. Get familiar and confident with using it. This confidence will allow you to concentrate on your delivery.

In technical presentations, be aware of problems with technical visuals. You may have to explain what a graph or diagram represents before explaining its meaning. Be especially careful about defining technical symbols whenever some audience members may not be familiar with them. On some occasions, you may have audience members who do not understand logarithmic graphs, for example. There are still countless people to whom the word *delta* is not the symbol for change, but the name of an airline. Long before *RAM* became the acronym for random access memory, it was the only way we could name a male member of the sheep family.

Here are some tips exclusively for handling overhead transparency and 35mm projection.

Presenting with Overhead Transparencies

The overhead projector is not easy to use effectively. Most presenters fail to exploit its advantages. Mastery requires a combination of planning, manual dexterity, and an awareness of several details. Here are some pointers that can help you use the overhead projector effectively.

It takes time to change overhead transparencies. You must remove the old visual from the projector, place it in the stack of used transparencies, then pick up the new visual, place it on the projector, and make sure it is framed properly. No matter how skillfully you change visuals, the audience experiences several seconds of what broadcasters refer to as "dead air." Nothing is happening. You can overcome dead air by providing *transitions* between visuals. *Don't stop talking when changing visuals.* The silence only accentuates the void in the presentation. Summarize the points in the departing visual or introduce the material coming up in the new one, or do both.

Use slip sheets between the transparencies, otherwise static electricity can cause them to cling together. Slip sheets make transparencies easy to handle. After you finish with each transparency, remove it from the projector and place it, along with its slip sheet, in a separate pile.

Try using a photocopy of the transparency as a slip sheet. You can jot down notes on the slip sheet that will help you remember the key points of a diagram, flow chart, illustration, or other graphic visual. Use just a few key points, otherwise you will be spending too much time reading. Print with large, black letters for visibility. During the presentation, place the transparency on the projector and hold its slip sheet in your hand. Move back until you are not blocking anyone's view of the screen. Glance down at the slip sheet to get your cues. When you are finished with the visual, move forward to the projector, remove the transparency, and place it and its slip sheet in the "used" pile, place the next transparency on the projector, and pick up the new slip sheet. This sounds complicated, but it isn't. Try it. It is just as easy to glance down at the slip sheet as it is the transparency.

We have referred often to the problem of standing without blocking anyone's view of the screen. With overhead transparencies, the standard position is to stand next to and just to the rear of the projector. You get your cues directly from the transparency. If the standard position obstructs someone's view of the screen, you have three options:

1. Sit down. (Not a good idea unless the audience is limited to three or four people.)
2. Move back beside the screen. Use a long pointer (35mm-style) and get your cues from the screen.
3. Have the slip sheets that separate each of your transparencies made up as photocopies, as suggested above.

Avoid looking too often or too long at the screen. At most, look once after you place each transparency on the projector to be sure all the image is on the screen. As you glance downward to pick up your cues, lower your eyes, not your head. Spend as much time as possible making eye contact with your audience.

Once the visual is on the projector, do not touch it until you remove it.

Use a pencil or pen to point out only important features in the visual. Lay the pencil on the visual. If you hold it, the slightest shaking of your hand will be magnified on the screen. You may also use a grease pencil or water-based marker to underline or circle key points and to write on the transparency.

Let's assume you have a visual that makes six complex points. To help your audience focus its attention on one point at a time, you cover the overhead transparency with a piece of paper so that only the first point is visible on the screen. The bottom of the screen is black. How do you think your audience will react to your cover-up? They dislike it. They resent your hiding material from them. They feel you are treating them like children—that you don't trust them with all the information. Beyond that serious problem, you have to uncover each point by carefully moving the sheet of paper. It's easy to uncover too much or not enough information—easy to find yourself fussing with a sheet of paper. What's the point? *Don't do it!* It is easier and infinitely more elegant to make six visuals, each one adding the next point while displaying all the points that have been covered previously.

Presenting with 35mm Slides

Here are several pointers to help you use the 35mm projector skillfully:

- Stand next to the screen if possible, pointer in the hand next to the screen and slide control unit in the other.
- Avoid optical pointers. They shine an image—usually an arrow—on the screen. Optical pointers are difficult to use and it takes a rock-steady hand to keep the arrow from jiggling wildly.
- Glance over at the screen to pick up your cues, then return immediately to eye contact with your audience. *Do not deliver your presenta-*

tion to the screen. If you point to something, hold the pointer in contact with the screen and look at the audience (not at the spot you are pointing to).

- Some people prefer to use an assistant to advance the slides. To have the sharpest timing, to avoid miscues and allow flexibility, operate your own slide control. Of course, the pointer and slide control will keep both hands occupied, but you will have total control over the visual channel. Taping the slide control unit to the lectern or table will work well, if you want one free hand.
- Do not totally darken the room. The audience should see you. You are an important part of the visual channel. In a totally dark room, the visuals dominate the presentation. Moreover, your audience cannot take notes. Also, dark rooms induce sleep. Modern presentation rooms have dimmers to control the light levels. Darken the room just enough to be able to see the colors in the slides vividly.

Nonprojected Media

The same rules apply to using flipcharts, easel pads, chalkboards, and other nonprojected media. Avoid distractions, be sure everyone can see the visual, face the audience, use a pointer, and use transitions between visuals.

Preparation

With a little practice you can master the few techniques that will help you use visuals with finesse and confidence. The more carefully you prepare, the more you can control the visual channel with smoothness and skill, and the less you will need to divert your attention away from your main purpose, communicating with your audience.

Using a Lectern

The word itself should be a warning to you. *Lectern* is from the Latin word for *reading.* The dictionary defines a lectern as a "reading desk." We both know at this stage that reading to an audience is unthinkable!

Lecterns pose several problems. First, they stand between you and your audience. This isolates you and prevents your getting close. Second, the audience can see only your upper torso and head. This view is not terribly interesting; it is a lot like watching a "head shot" on television for an hour. Third, the lectern tends to inhibit *all* movement. Many speakers clutch the top edges of the lectern with a fierce tenacity. Gestures become as rare as items you can buy for a nickel. Fourth, it is too easy for the lectern to become a crutch. You feel comfortable behind there with your notes and your glass of water, and maybe a microphone so you can speak normally. If you grow too accustomed to using a lectern, your first presentation without it can become a frightening experience.

If you do use a lectern for a *presentation*, use it only to hold your notes and glass of water. Spend your time speaking *beside* the lectern. Even better, be familiar enough with your material so that you can come away from the lectern (at least come out a few feet) and return to it for your next cue. In a normal presentation (not a speech), your cues should be on the screen, not in a stack of notes. Use the lectern as a reference table.

Lecterns are useful for reading speeches; more on that later.

Using a Microphone

If you can, choose a *wireless* mike. It allows you to move around the room without being concerned about tripping on or pulling wires. If you use a neck microphone, you must become adept at managing (not tripping over) the cord. The third, and least desirable, type is the fixed microphone. Fixed microphones not only immobilize you, they also cause other problems. If you turn or pull away (for example, to look at the screen briefly), the sound level falls off. Your audience can't hear you. It takes enormous presence of mind and discipline to keep your mouth exactly eight inches from a fixed microphone and still do all of the other things a presentation requires. Often the microphone can be removed from its cradle. If you can do this and still have enough extra cord to move about, try holding the microphone in your hand.

One of the most annoying—and frequent—problems with public address systems is the squeal caused when sound from the loudspeakers feeds back to the microphone. Be sure to check the PA system before the presentation. If feedback howl occurs during the presentation, try to point the microphone away from the speaker(s), or have someone point the speakers away from the mike. It also can help to move the microphone further from your mouth.

TONE

Part of your delivery style is your overall *tone*. Your tone is how you impress an audience—how you *seem* to them. Your tone can be cheerful, friendly, stern, serious, tentative, aggressive, grave, sarcastic, mocking, paternalistic, insulting, warm, cool, aloof, withdrawn, passionate, officious, formal, challenging, combative, defensive, helpful, "take-it-or-leave-it," or even neutral. Tone is composed of your facial expressions (or the lack of them), your posture and body movements, your choice of words (formal vs. informal, objective vs. slanted, cerebral vs. emotional), and the *paralinguistics* of your speech, that is, *how* you say your words. Indeed, virtually every element of delivery we have discussed contributes to the overall tone of your delivery.

Take one small example: smiling. Often an inexperienced speaker, because of the pressure to do well, or because of being a bit nervous, will never smile. The overall tone becomes one of grave seriousness. Smiling, too, requires a balanced approach. If you are addressing the problems of nuclear fallout, your audience is likely to misinterpret repeated smiling. If you never smile, however, you are considered a grouch. On the other hand, if you smile all the time, people tend to think you're a simpering idiot.

In mastering all the elements of effective delivery, you should strive for a tone that is confident, positive, sincere, friendly, and authoritative; confident without being cocky, positive without being a cheerleader, sincere without being "goody-goody," friendly without being too chummy, and authoritative without being a know-it-all.

When delivering a presentation, be aware that you are communicating on many levels. Having an engaging tone helps to create a resonance between you and your audience and helps to build and maintain rapport.

HANDLING QUESTIONS

We now turn to one of the most vital—often most overlooked—facets of delivery: the skill of handling questions and conducting a discussion with an audience. It is possible to undermine the gains of an otherwise excellent presentation by an inept handling of the questions and comments of your audience. On the brighter side, when an audience is only marginally in agreement with you, the question-and-answer session can tip the scales in favor of achieving your objective.

Q&A sessions serve a variety of useful purposes:

- To ensure that the audience understands your subject
- To provide more detail on certain points
- To deal with concerns or doubts on specific arguments
- To provide a forum for airing problems and/or frustrations
- To allow an exchange of views and ideas among audience members

Q&A sessions help the presenter gauge the audience's reaction to the presentation—both the level of understanding and the level of acceptance. Many pitfalls lie in the path of the presenter in these sessions. The next few pages will help you avoid the major blunders as well as the minor flubs.

When Do You Want Questions?

Decide if you wish your audience to ask questions during the presentation or hold them until it is completed. Questions asked during the presentation help to clarify confusion or resolve doubts as they arise. In certain kinds of presentations, audience participation is necessary—for example, in a presentation whose objective is to collectively solve a problem. In this case, it is vital that everyone understand the complexities of the problem at every stage of the explanation.

But questions asked during the presentation also can cause problems. As the questions and the discussions pile up, your presentation can eventually turn into a meeting. It takes a good deal of skill to keep the engine on the tracks and to avoid spending time on minor points, especially if the audience is composed of high-level executives. It is not unusual, under these conditions, to run out of time before being able to finish. Another problem is that often a question is asked whose answer will occur later in the presentation. The options are to either leave your outline to cover the material out of sequence or to explain, "I'll be covering that point a little later on." Neither choice is especially palatable.

Whether you decide to deal with questions during your presentation or after it, *tell* your audience at the outset; let them know your wishes. One way to postpone questions is to provide everyone with a pad and pencil. Number the visuals. Explain to your audience that you want them to hold their questions and why. Follow that with something like, "Please jot your questions down along with the number of the visual. I'll cover all your questions after I get through the material I have prepared for you."

For many presentations, the best strategy is to adopt a middle ground between holding all questions at one extreme and stopping to answer every question and field every comment on the other. It goes something like this:

> It is critical that we make it through *all* the material I have before we begin the discussion. There will be sufficient time to deal with all your concerns. It is also vital that each of you understands the information we have to cover. So, in the interests of everyone, please hold your comments and discussion points until the end. But if you don't *understand* something, please *interrupt* me for clarification. (The word "interrupt" was carefully chosen.)

Whatever your strategy for postponing questions, you must still be prepared for interruptions. This is especially true if the audience is composed of high-ranking executives, who usually speak their piece no matter what ground rules you attempt to establish. Should you be interrupted, simply deal with the question or comment and return immediately to your presentation. Do not give the impression you wish to continue answering questions. Answer quickly and briefly with a sense of finality in your voice. Confine your answer to the questioner, and do not look at anyone else.

Keep in mind, however, that the objective is never to give a presentation. The presentation is a means for achieving an objective. If you are interrupted, by all means be flexible. In some cases, answering questions and *conducting* a discussion will accomplish your objective as readily as will a formal presentation. If you have prepared thoroughly, your ideas and arguments will prevail in either format. Remember to defend your ideas without seeming to be defensive or combative. Give people the opportunity to express doubts and concerns. Be careful not to rush prematurely for agreement or closure.

Your preparation should always include an analysis of the questions you are likely to be asked—*especially the difficult questions.* Of course, you can't predict every conceivable question, but by becoming your own critic, you can anticipate most of them. The goal is not simply to be ready for specific questions; it is to prepare the most convincing and illuminating answers.

So much for the preliminaries. Here are some guidelines for handling questions.

Q&A Should Be a Group Process

Just as a presentation involves every audience member, so should the Q&A session. Do not engage in a series of conversations with individuals, but instead be certain that the audience shares both the questions and the answers.

With audiences larger than 20 or so, or in acoustically difficult rooms, some people cannot hear every question. Untrained speakers are seldom aware that audience members usually ask questions in their social communications zone, not the group zone. Have you ever been in a large audience, unable to hear some of the questions? Do you remember what it was like to try to reason what the questions were to the answers you were hearing? Annoying, isn't it?

Develop the skill of judging whether everyone *hears* every question. At the beginning of the Q&A session, it is helpful to ask, "Did everyone hear the question?" Not only will you get a better feel for minimum acceptable volume, your audience members are likely to speak louder. The best solution is simply to repeat the question, but only when you suspect not everyone heard it. It is bad form to ask the questioner to repeat it (unless you didn't hear it yourself). Also bad form is asking an individual questioner to *speak up; we can't hear you!* It is acceptable to ask the entire audience—especially at the beginning of the Q&A session—to be aware that, unless they speak up, others in the room will not hear their questions.

Having assured that everyone hears the question, next be certain that everyone *understands* it. Audience members possess different levels of understanding. If you are asked a highly technical question, take time to define new terms or to explain unfamiliar material before and during the answer.

Finally, you should maintain a group process by *sharing the answer with the entire audience.* Don't respond only to the questioner; that traps you into excluding the rest of your audience. Begin your answer by looking at the questioner for a few seconds, then break away, and resume your normal delivery techniques. Answer to the entire audience. Return frequently to the questioner with your eyes, but continue to deliver the answer to everyone.

Take Your Time

You will often know how you will answer a question long before the questioner has finished asking it. Never communicate that fact. Always hear the entire question, then wait a second or so before answering it. Pausing before answering has two benefits: First, it avoids the embarrassment of cutting off the questioner who may not quite have finished; second, it gives the impression that you are considering the question.

Don't rush through your answer. This can create the impression that you want to get the Q&A session over, especially if you seem impatient (e.g., glancing at your watch). Answer the question as carefully and completely as you can. If you suspect the questioner did not understand the answer, or that the answer did not satisfy the question, *test* to find out. Either ask, "Does that answer your question?" or simply glance at the questioner and seek nonverbal confirmation. Do not just rush to the next question, assuming you have cleared up the matter.

Do's and Don'ts for Handling Questions

Do's

- If you do not understand the question, say so. You are not expected to be telepathic. Ask for more information or begin your answer by testing your understanding of the question. "Do you mean . . .?"
- Do treat every question as legitimate and well-intentioned, even if you suspect it may be designed to trip you up or be destructive.
- Do answer the question directly. Avoid digressions. Get to the point.
- Do be friendly, helpful, and concerned that each questioner understands your answer. Recognize the difference between understanding your answer and agreeing with it. If your questioner wishes to debate, you must decide when to move on to the next question. Can something be gained by debating the issue? Each situation is different. In some cases, it makes sense to assure the answer is understood and then move on, because the remainder of your audience accepts the answer or the format is not one of debate, but rather, of clarification. On other occasions, it may be vital that all objections, concerns, and disagreements are thoroughly explored.

- Do answer an inappropriate question directly by explaining that "that question is out of my area of expertise" or "not within the scope of this study," for example.
- Do go back to an appropriate visual if it will help make your answer clearer or save time.
- Use humor when appropriate. Let the audience know that you don't take yourself too seriously. A *sprinkling* of humor can relax you and your audience. Just don't overdo it. Use one-liners and avoid five-minute shaggy dog stories.

Don'ts

- Don't try to bluff your way through an answer. If you do not know the answer, say so. But follow up by asking the questioner to see you after the session is over so that you may arrange to provide the answer requested. If you are discovered in the act of faking an answer, your credibility quotient drops to zero!
- Don't browbeat a questioner, of course.
- Don't extract humor at the expense of the questioner. No matter how harmless you may think the humor is, the questioner or someone else in the audience may take offense. That someone else may not ask an important question because of your earlier humorous barb.
- Don't indicate that you covered the material earlier. This only serves to embarrass the questioner. Don't even try to do it apologetically: "I guess *when I covered that earlier* I didn't explain it as carefully as I should have." Such attempts only heighten the questioner's discomfort at having asked a question about something that has already been covered. Just answer the question.
- Don't answer the question with another question. The Socratic Method is inappropriate in presentations. So too are impertinent rejoinders such as "Well, what do *you* think it means?" You are there to provide answers.
- Don't comment on the question: "Good question!" "I'm glad you asked that question." "Thank you for asking that question." "What a marvelous question." These clichés waste time. More important, if you use them too often, you sound insincere. After a long series of "good question" comments, if you answer a question without comment, you imply the question is substandard or lacking merit.
- Don't use expressions such as "frankly," "to be honest," "to tell the truth," "to be perfectly candid" when answering. These may be natural responses in conversations, but in the more formal setting of a presentation, such comments suggest that you haven't been "perfectly

candid" until this moment. Even in everyday conversation, such expressions can be harmful.

- Don't unexpectedly call on someone else to answer your question. Your audience may contain experts whose assistance with a question may be invaluable. Asking for help is perfectly acceptable if it is done correctly. For example, "There may be someone here who wishes to add to or improve upon my answer. Please feel free to help us out." (Pause) Never toss the question to someone: "Charlie has had considerable experience in this area; I'm sure he could explain it much more expertly than I." Poor Charlie. He was sitting comfortably over there in the corner minding his own business, enjoying the presentation. Suddenly he is thrust onto center stage. He must collect and organize his thoughts to speak to 30 people as an expert. A better, more humane method is to see Charlie *before* the presentation and ask for his help, should you need it. Be as specific as possible about the information you wish him to be available to provide. Your audience may contain several "experts" whose help you have sought in advance.

Special Challenges

Q&A sessions are enjoyable because they are unpredictable. There is no script, only a plan. And things don't always go according to plan.

You may not get *any* questions. It takes a bit of courage to ask a question in front of an audience. Many people do not enjoy calling attention to themselves. Then there is the risk of asking a dumb question in front of your peers, colleagues, or superiors. Sometimes the sheer size of an audience inhibits questions.

Here are three ways to help get questions. First, ask in a way that convinces audiences that you really want to answer their questions, then *wait*. Use a little humor while you are waiting, but give them time to come up with something. Eventually, some fearless soul will venture forth. Usually after that first question is answered (skillfully, of course, by you), several hands will shoot up. If waiting does not work, use your own starter questions. Begin by explaining that several important questions are worth exploring, or that in previous presentations, several common questions have emerged. Ask the first question, then answer it. Incidentally, planting questioners in the audience to ask prepared starter questions not only seems dishonest, it is unnecessary! The third method is to hand out blank 3-by-5-inch cards at the beginning of the presentation. Ask audience members to jot down their questions during the presentation. Explain that the cards will be collected at the end and the questions answered. Questioners can remain anonymous and out of the spotlight. This third method works well with large audiences (more than 40 or 50 people).

E Pluribus Unum. This phrase, "Out of many, one," should not prevail during presentations. The Q&A period should not be dominated by one person. The audience becomes restless, impatient, irritated. Your job is to maintain control and give all who wish to an opportunity to participate.

Here are a few problem cases and some suggestions on how to deal with them:

- *The speechmaker* doesn't really have a question, but wants to comment extensively on everything. It is always best to avoid cutting anyone off. Begin by asking the speechmaker, "Do you have a question?" After a reasonable period for the expression of the person's views, you must go on to another question. Try, "Let's see if there are any *others* who may have questions."

- *The zealot* is so interested and enthused about your subject that he or she is not aware that others are being denied time. Try calling on other people in preference to the zealot. If the problem becomes too severe, try something like, "You seem especially interested in this subject. Rather than taking *everyone's* time here, let's meet afterward so that I can give you the degree of detail you need. Thank you."

- *The helper* is never quite satisfied with your answers and is compelled to interpret and amplify each one. It is a way of showing one's brilliance, or simply how well informed one is, under the guise of being helpful. You may have to tell the helper that the assistance is not wanted. Much depends, of course, on just how much help you are getting. It is only the compulsive helper who is a problem.

- *The comedian* enjoys using the Q&A session to stage a performance. When you get a question whose real purpose is not to get an answer, but to get a laugh, enjoy it. When the same person does it a *second* time, enjoy it a little less (depends on how good the material is). Do not enjoy the third rouser at all. Look away from the comedian and ask the rest of the audience, "Does anyone have a question?" Remember, you are in charge. The audience expects you to *conduct* the presentation. It is possible to enjoy a sprinkling of humor without having the Q&A session deteriorate into a burlesque show.

- *The boor* is a person who will not pay attention. The boor does paperwork or reads while you are conducting the presentation—the boor's reading program can even include newspapers and magazines! The world-class boor, however, is one who *distracts the audience* by talking—often loudly—to others in the vicinity. It is hard to imagine anything more rude. Sleeping is a far kinder, more civilized behavior. Your first tactic is to single out and draw in the boor. Ask if he or she has a question, or something that could be shared with the rest of the audience. That's a gentle way of letting the boor know that you wish either participation or silence. You should be warned, however, that this will not even slow down a world-class boor. If you must escalate, try this: "I would really appreciate it if we could have one meeting. There will be plenty of time for discussions after I get through the presentation. Thank you." If this polite request is ineffective, you have a more powerful—and riskier—next step. A more severe measure is to point out to the boorish one (after trying steps one and two, above) that he or she is disrupting the presentation, and that you can appreciate that the conversation they are having must really be urgent, but could it be conducted in another room, so that the rest of the audience can concentrate on the presentation? This last step is riskier if the disruptive person is also someone who has some influence on you in your organization—especially economic influence. Those of you who cherish gainful employment may choose not to invoke that last step.

- **The heckler** diverts audience attention and frustrates the entire communication process by becoming the raucus opposite pole of the presenter. Hecklers are so rare in business and technical presentations that it scarcely seems necessary to mention the subject. If you should encounter one, however, remember: You are in charge. The audience becomes just as irritated with the heckler as you are. They expect you to speak up in their interest. Don't descend to the level of the heckler by attempting to trade barbs or sarcasm. Take a professional, businesslike approach. Indicate that the kind of comment is not appreciated, and that it does nothing to illuminate the discussion.

Remember that whoever asks a question does so as a representative of the entire audience. Treat that person with care. If one person dominates the proceedings, however, that person eventually loses his or her audience membership card. You can see and hear the signs of rejection. The audience begins to tell you, "Take care of this problem so that we can get on with our business."

Another challenge you should be prepared for is ending a Q&A session when you do not have time to answer every question. This rarely happens in a business or technical presentation, but occasionally, with very large audiences it can pose a problem. One of the best ways to handle it is to explain that not enough time remains to answer every question, that you will answer *three* more. Answer the next question, then announce, "Two more." After answering, announce, "Last question."

A final word of advice: Q&A sessions are full of surprises, unexpected twists, frustrations, and delights. Be ready for anything, and no matter what happens, never lose your composure.

PUTTING IT ALL TOGETHER

Remember the last time you saw a really effective speaker? Quite likely that speaker was combining all the elements we have discussed and was aiming at one goal: making contact with each member of that audience.

The voice reaching out to the audience filled the space you were in. The vocal delivery was smooth, without unexpected stops. Words came at a pace that helped you concentrate without effort. The voice was full of vitality and energy. Pauses and changes of pace and animation made listening to the voice a pleasure. Beyond the voice, remember the speaker's eyes, facial expressions, hands—the entire body—was working to engage you in the verbal and nonverbal messages, to create between you a *resonance*, a relationship that helped you share ideas and attitudes.

Good delivery means *engaging* an audience, making contact by using the *energy* within you to reach out and fill the space with your voice and body. Good delivery requires *empathy*, the ability to think and feel as one with your audience, the ability to see and hear the signals they send, and the skill to react to them. Good delivery means establishing a rapport with your audience and encouraging a climate that encourages asking questions and taking risks. It means dealing with questions in a way that involves everyone in the audience. Good delivery does not mean mastering a list of actor's tricks. In fact, good actors are expert in convincing us they are somebody else. Good delivery is being yourself, allowing your natural style to emerge—two things that add up to the big difference between merely talking to an audience and communicating with one.

In the last analysis, good delivery is a collection of nuances. Most audiences are not sensitive to them; they just know what good delivery is when they experience it. Your part is to develop an awareness of these nuances, become sensitive to them in your delivery style and practice. As with so many things, perfection is in the details.

11

Other Thoughts

Before we part company, let's talk about several special applications related to presentations.

A DRY RUN

One important way to improve a presentation is to have one or more practice runs. Dry runs of business or technical presentations are the exception, not the rule, because they are time consuming and expensive. They are conducted when the stakes justify it. If you cannot afford anything *less* than a razor sharp, highly polished performance, the best way to assure it is the dry run.

Here are some pointers for getting the most out of a dry run.

- Schedule the practice run far enough in advance to be able to make necessary changes.
- As much as possible, duplicate the conditions of the final presentation. Go to the actual room where it will be held. Use the same audiovisual equipment, visuals, and public address system, if applicable.
- Use a live audience—a special audience of critics who are carefully selected and prepared to provide feedback.
- Explain to your audience beforehand that you want their reactions to the presentation on the following:
  —The clarity of the information. Did everyone understand the material?

—The soundness and the persuasiveness of the arguments.
—The effectiveness of the visuals. Were they clear? legible? easy to follow? balanced? appropriate?
—The effectiveness of the delivery.
—The organization and flow of information. Was it easy to follow, or did it suffer from confusing missteps?
—Were the issues clearly drawn?
—Were the action alternatives or the recommendations clearly and emphatically set forth?
—What was the overall tone of the presentation?

- Also tell the dry run audience that you want to ask questions during and after the presentation. You will need their evaluation of the answers you gave as well.
- Appoint an official timer. Be sure that the *speaking portion* of the presentation is timed as well as the total elapsed time. The timer should extract time used to comment on and improve the presentation, but include real questions and discussion of the subject. The goal is to get a reasonably accurate feel for whether or not the presentation can be completed in its allotted time.

Take notes during the critique. Use the information to perfect the content by improving the organization, explanations, arguments, visuals, and timing of the presentation. Use the comments to polish your delivery techniques.

FOUR METHODS OF ADDRESSING AN AUDIENCE

The four classical methods are these:

1. *Impromptu*—You are asked to speak with no warning and no real opportunity to prepare.
2. *Extemporaneous*—Delivering a prepared speech from *notes* or an audiovisual presentation. In both cases, the speaker is not locked into and dependent on specific wording. The speaker covers the material in whatever words come to mind.
3. *Reading a Speech from a Manuscript*
4. *Delivering a Speech from Memory*

This book has dealt extensively with the second method. The fourth method is rarely used in business and technical circles. However, we should spend some time discussing impromptu speaking and giving a speech from manuscript. These two methods are by no means rare.

GIVING AN IMPROMPTU SPEECH

An impromptu speech is one in which a speaker is asked to say a few words, either on short notice, or with no notice at all. This situation always produces less than polished results. In fact, it is well to remember that the audience does not expect carefully turned phrases and highly refined commentary. On nearly every occasion, they are looking for an answer to the question, "What do *you* think?" They expect you will answer the question in the best off-the-cuff way you can. Should you be called on to deliver an impromptu speech, follow these guides to help you meet the challenge.

- Don't get caught flat-footed. If you suspect that you may be called to speak, prepare for it from the beginning of the meeting. Take notes on the highlights. Jot down the telling points and the people who made them. Most important, relate the material to your experience and capture *your reactions.*
- Form your opinions as the meeting progresses. Be prepared to defend them. Use key, trigger words only in your notes. If you create volumes of writing, it won't help you when you have to speak.
- If you are called on, begin with a summary of your impressions. Don't hurry. Use the time to decide on the points you wish to make. Remember, impromptu speeches are informal. Use simple, familiar, conversational words.
- Use your best delivery techniques.
- Use the remarks of other speakers as departures for making or emphasizing your points.
- Develop a good closer, or emphatic way of summarizing your remarks.
- If you *are* caught totally by surprise, take time to collect your thoughts. Relate the topic to your own experiences and opinions. Above all, be brief. Do not mumble on. Simply make the two or three points you find worth making, then, with a smile, a nod, or a gesture toward the moderator, take your seat.

READING A SPEECH

It is difficult to read a speech to an audience with spontaneity and feeling. Audiences generally find it boring when they are read to in the manner used by untrained speakers. If you must deliver a speech from a manuscript, you might as well do it effectively. Here are some pointers on doing just that.

- If you are writing the speech, begin by creating an outline. Organize your thoughts for maximum impact and clarity.
- Rather than writing your speech, try speaking into a recording device

for a first draft. Your speech is likely to sound much more spontaneous and conversational. Have the recording transcribed onto paper and edit the draft later. (Just don't edit out all of the spontaneity.)

- If you write your speech, remember the difference between writing and talking. Use short, familiar, conversational words and avoid "businessese" or "technicalese" language. Use short sentences, but be aware that an endless succession of short, staccato sentences will eventually lull your audience to sleep. Mix in longer sentences, but make them easy for the listener to follow. You should be able to speak your sentences as you would in a normal conversation.

- Have the speech typed with letters large enough for you to be able to read in dim light. Use upper- and lowercase letters as long as the type is easy to read, otherwise use all capital letters. Triple space the lines. Have two-inch margins on either side of the text. Use the margins to make notes for ad libs or short departures from your text to improve spontaneity.

- Instead of typing the text in paragraph form, type it in phrases. When we speak, we link words into phrases we can say in a single breath. If each word is said as a unit, the speech lacks emphasis, and is boring. For example, John Kennedy would *not* have captivated us with:

> Ask
> not
> what
> your
> country
> can
> do
> for
> you.
> Ask
> what
> you
> can
> do
> for
> your
> country.

A more effective way to type those lines might be...

> Ask NOT
> what your COUNTRY can do for YOU.
> Ask what YOU can do for your COUNTRY.

- Go over your speech carefully. What are the salient points you wish your audience to remember? What action do you wish them to take? How do you want to change their views? Plan the ways in which you will make these points stand out in your delivery.
- We emphasize important words by giving them more volume, more time, or more animation. Mark the words you wish to emphasize, either by underlining them with a marker or in some typographic way. Mark pauses with ellipses (. . .). Mark the places where you will use more or less animation with up and down arrows.
- Rehearse your speech. Do it *aloud*. Practice your phrasing, emphasis, pace, timing, animation. Get comfortable with how you sound. If you prefer, practice in front of someone who can give you a candid reaction. Time your speech.
- The most important element in reading a speech is to make it seem that you are not reading. It may help you to imagine you are speaking normally to one person. You must be so familiar with the speech that you can look away from it and return to it smoothly. Remember, the ideas of the speech are what are important, not the words. If you choose a similar word to the one in your text occasionally, so be it. When you glance down at your manuscript, do not lower your head, just your eyes. Spend as much time as possible looking at people, not simply staring into the middle distance. Whatever you do, strive to sound natural and spontaneous. Some speakers even add an occasional "um" to the delivery to make it sound more human.

TEAM PRESENTATIONS

Team presentations are a natural outgrowth of team efforts. For example, in the development of a new product, different groups may be responsible for various parts of the total effort: the mechanical, electronic, optical, software, packaging, design teams—each knows the complex details of its own contribution better than any individual can know them for all groups. Thus, team technical presentations for reporting on major programs involving many disciplines are quite common. Similarly, team presentations are used in business presentations when the efforts of contributing groups need to be communicated individually. The format usually involves using one person on the presentation team to communicate the part with which he or she is most familiar. Another potent advantage of the team approach can occur in the Q&A session, when each presenter on the team joins to form a panel of experts, which can handle both the breadth and the depth of questions likely to come from the audience.

One of the pitfalls of team presentations, however, is a lack of overall coordination and unity. Team members, left to their own devices, tend to present their own material in their own way, without much—if any—concern for the continuity and the overall effect of the *entire* presentation.

Here are several ideas for perfecting team presentations.

- Designate an overall planner/director to work with each team member in developing the purpose, scope, message, the outline, script, level of detail, and the method of presentation. The overall planner helps to design the format for the entire presentation and is concerned about continuity, unity, and emphasis.
- The overall planner must always take the point of view of the audience: How does the presentation flow? How does each team member's presentation link with its predecessor and build into the next segment? Are there any gaps? What are the overriding impressions the audience is left with?
- The overall plan should include an introduction, usually given by the person responsible for the work of all the team members. The same person usually delivers a conclusion or summary after the last team member finishes, then opens the Q&A session.
- Another technique is to use a respected member of the organization who has highly developed delivery and audience communication skills as a "master of ceremonies." The MC delivers the introduction, introduces each of the team presenters at the appropriate time, and presents the summary or conclusion.
- Each team member need not use the same kind of visuals, although doing so vastly simplifies the production of the overall presentation. Avoid using documents or working drawings for visuals.
- The middle speakers confine their presentations to their own material. In some formats they introduce the next speaker.
- Avoid using two people to present concurrently, that is, interweaving their lines. It takes professional actors to get the timing correct. It is almost impossible to perform successfully.
- Delivery skills are even more important in team presentations than in solo efforts. Why? Because the audience compares the speakers. If one person is conspicuously behind the other team members, try to get that person some professional coaching.
- Be certain that one person has the the responsibility for coordinating all of the production details: facility, visuals, audiovisual equipment, lighting, sound system, etc.

DELIVERING AN INTRODUCTION

Anyone can deliver an introduction, right? Not really. It's one of those minor art forms that few people study and most people take for granted. Here's a checklist for review the next time you have the opportunity to introduce a speaker.

- *Be brief.* You are not the speaker. Your job is to get the speaker launched as quickly and successfully as possible. The audience very quickly becomes impatient when the introduction goes beyond a minute or two. Don't wander from the topic; stick to business.
- Spend a little time with the speaker beforehand. Learn what you need to know about the speaker's background and the message to be conveyed.
- Begin the introduction by establishing the speaker's credentials, but without listing a boring resume. Limit yourself to the speaker's significant achievements in the subject area. Don't exaggerate the speaker's qualifications or build unrealistic expectations.
- Introduce the topic. Establish a linkage between the audience and the speaker. What special information can the speaker give? Why is the topic important to them? How will your audience benefit?
- Don't compete with the speaker with flashes of brilliance.
- Don't get into the speaker's material or give away any of the speaker's points.
- Never apologize for anything! If the speaker is a last-minute substitute, don't call that to anyone's attention in your introduction. Don't make your audience aware that the speaker has not had the usual amount of time to prepare. The introduction is no place for negatives or apologies.

One last thing to remember: Never leave the podium until the speaker is almost in place and ready to speak. If the speaker is coming in from off stage or from the audience, wait until he or she arrives and is nearly in place to speak. You may wish to ask for a greeting of applause and to shake the speaker's hand, but now it is time for you to retire unobtrusively.

Nice job.

PRESENTATIONS BY HANDICAPPED PERSONS

If you have ever wondered if a person can deliver an effective presentation from a wheelchair, the answer is an emphatic "yes." The principles of vocal delivery and gestures can be mastered by speakers with special challenges of numerous sorts. Not surprisingly, one of the most effective presentations I have seen was given by a speaker who is legally blind. The important thing is to practice and perfect your skills.

USING VIDEOTAPE

Videotaping equipment is probably the best tool available for improving your delivery. It gives you the opportunity to become your own audience. Be prepared for the shock of seeing and hearing yourself for the first time—the camera adds 15 pounds and 10 years. Once you overcome video shock, you can evaluate your voice, posture, movements—your entire delivery technique as an audience member would. Seeing yourself is immediate and much more powerful than getting reactions secondhand from others.

Another advantage of videotape is the ability to replay and study portions of your presentation. The best of all possible worlds is to videotape a dry run then review the tape with the dry-run audience.

THE VALUE OF PREPARATION

Delivering the presentation is only about 5 percent of the total work. Delivery requires speaking the words and showing the images that were selected, designed, and prepared well in advance of the moment of delivery. Never underestimate the value of preparation. Quite often, we underestimate the amount of time we will need to spend away from our normal duties until it is too late. The overall professional impact of the presentation is a direct result of analysis, planning, design, care, effort. More often than not, a poor presentation is the result of inadequate preparation. The most expensive commodity is time. There is almost never enough.

LUCK

A conventional way to close would be to wish you good luck, but by now we both know that successful presentations are not a matter of luck at all.

Things that have a lot to do with successful presentations include attention to detail, being audience-centered, being able to think like another person, being logical, analyzing arguments and motivation, sharing, making contact, taking risks, desire, work, imagination, craftsmanship—but luck has very little to do with it.

My closing wish is that you accomplish your objectives, whatever they may be.

Index

Abbreviations, 64
Accents, 154
Acoustic space, 146
Acoustics, 119
Acronyms, 64
Adversaries, 34
Agenda slide, 71-72
Alcoholic beverages, 125
Analogy, 53
Analysis, 49
Animation, 149-150, 154
Apologizing, 134, 135, 136, 154
Appearance, 141, 162-163
Appointments, 4
Argument, 25, 54, 55
Articulation, 151-153
Asides, 136
Audience
  attitudes, 25
  dissimilar backgrounds, 24, 25
  feedback, 6, 7, 147, 155, 157
  member roles, 33
Audience analysis, 22-27
  technical presentations, 24

Audience-centeredness, 18, 38, 39, 133
Audiovisual
  equipment, 119, 121, 124, 127, 163-168
  services, 98, 99-100, 117
Audiovisual presentation, definition, 3

Balance between audio and visual
  channels, 87-89
Bar graphs, 103-109
Behavior, 17
Behavioral objectives, 18-20
Benefit to the audience, 41
Bluffing, 173
Boor, 175-176
Breaking from delivery, 135
Breaks, 126-127, 143, 157
Breathing, 136, 142
Bullets, 100
Business presentations, 5, 102

CAD drawings, 97, 112
Canned presentations, 79-80
Cause and effect, 49

Chairs, 125
Chalkboard, 81, 124, 164
Chart software, 95
Chronology, 49
Classification, 49
Coffee, 126, 142
Color
    rules for effective use, 115
    use in visuals, 86, 115
Colors, responses to, 113-115
Column charts, 103, 106, 107
Comedian, 69, 173, 175
Communication
    definition, 27
    desire, 29
    false assumption of, 28
    humility, 30
    and sharing, 28, 30
    work, 30
    zones, 145-146
Communications methods, hierarchical
        value, 4, 5
Company mail, 4
Computer generated
    graphics, 93-99
    outlines, 59, 95
    presentations, 81
Computer graphics software, 93-97
Computer pointing devices, 97
Control, 8
Copies of visuals as reference, 83
Credibility, 25, 35, 173
Cue cards, 73, 89, 100

Dead air, 165
Decision trees, 112
Deduction, 51
De-emphasizing the speaker, 26, 78
Definition
    audiovisual presentation, 4
    communication, 27
    extemporaneous speech, 179
    impromptu speech, 179
    meeting, 4
    organization, 39

    speech, 4
    visual, 73
Delivery
    pace, 146-148
    style, 131
Desire in communication, 29
Desktop presentations, 93
Deviation chart, 107
Diagrams, 111-113
Dialects, 154
Digitizing tablet, 97, 98
Dimmer, 78, 167
Discussion, 169-176
Distractions
    caused by the speaker, 161
    in the environment, 125, 161, 175
Documents for visuals, 86, 112
Dot matrix printer, 98
Draw software, 95
"Drop-by" meetings, 4
Drugs, 142
Dry run, 178-179

Easel pad, 82, 164
Editorializing, 136
Electronic images, 80-81
Electronic mail, 4
Electronic schematics, 112
Elimination, 53
Eliot, T.S., 30
Emotion, 55-56
Empathy, 72, 133, 144
Emphasis, 71
Energy, 132, 136, 142, 144, 146, 162
Engagement, 132, 143
Enhancement programs, 95
Entertainment in a presentation, 18
Enunciation, 151-153
Equipment checklist, 127
Exposition, 17, 48-51
Extemporaneous speech, 179
Eye contact, 155-157

Fanny factor, 126
Fear, 55, 137

Feedback
  acoustic, 120, 168
  audience, 6, 7, 147, 155, 157
Fight or flight, 137–138, 140
Flan recipe, 23
Flip charts, 82
Foam board, 82
Formality, 12–15, 18
  factors influencing, 13
Frame, 61, 70
Frame durations, 61, 84, 89
Frequency distributions, 109, 110

G & T case study, 43–48
Gain, 55
Gestures, 157–159
Graphics, 93–117

Handouts, 83
Hands, 157–159
Hard copy, 10
Hecklers, 176
Helper, 175
Herd instinct, 56
Histogram, 107
Hook, 57
Horizontal bar charts, 107
Humility in communication, 30
Humor, 69–70, 142

Idea density, 70, 147
Immediacy, 7
Impact, 7
Impromptu speech, 179, 180
Inclusion, 36, 42, 58
Induction, 52–53
Inductive leap, 52
Inflection, 149–150
Informal meetings, 4
Ink jet printer, 98
Input scanner, 97
Introducing a speaker, 184

Jargon, 63
Jewelry, 161, 163
Jokes, 69, 142

Keep going, 134–136, 144
Keystone effect, 76

Lantern slides, 79
Laser printers, 93, 98
Lavaliere microphone, 119
Learning, a three-part process, 8
Lecterns, 124, 167–168
Left brain, 103
Legibility of visuals, 86
Length of presentation, 125
Level of detail, 10, 23, 24, 64, 70
Light dimmer, 78, 167
Line graphs, 109–110
Liquid-crystal-display projection system,
  80
Listening, 8, 9
  barriers to, 144
Logic, 51, 55

Meeting, 4
Memorandum, 4, 86
Mental blank, overcoming, 143
Message, 27–28, 155
Microphone
  fixed, 119, 168
  hand-held, 168
  lavaliere, 119
  wireless, 119, 168
Mnemonics, 89
Mock-ups, 83, 116
Models, 83, 116
Monotone, 149, 154
Mountain graphs, 110
Mouse, 97–98
Movement, 160–162
Movies, 80

Negative information, 35
Nervousness, 136–143
  mental preparation, 139–141
  physical preparation, 141–143
Nonprojected media, 74, 81–84, 125, 167
Nonverbal communication, 9, 27, 147,
  155, 159, 163

Objective of presentation, 16–21, 25, 31
Objectives, realistic, 20
Opaque projector, 79
Organization, definition, 39
Organizational patterns
  analogy, 53
  analysis, 49
  cause and effect, 49
  chronology, 49
  classification, 49
  deduction, 51
  elimination, 53
  induction, 52–53
  question and answer, 49
  rebuttal, 54–55
  themes and subthemes, 42, 57–58
Outline, 39, 45–48, 72
Outlining techniques, 57–59
Output devices, 93, 98
Overcommunication, 24
Overhead transparency, 75–77, 82, 86, 109, 165–166
Overloading the channels, 88
Overqualification, 67–68

Pace, 11, 70, 146–148, 154
Paint software, 95
Paper
  bond, 92
  office copier, 92
  sulphite, 92
Paralinguistics, 7, 149, 150, 168
Pass-outs, 83
Pauses, 148–149
Perfection, quest for, 130–131
Personal credibility, 25, 35, 173
Persuasion, 16, 48, 51–56
PERT diagrams, 112
Phone calls, 4, 5
Photographs, 77, 116, 117
Physical factors, 118–128
Pie charts, 110–111
Piping diagrams, 112
Pneumatic schematics, 112
Podium, 184

Pointers, 124, 164, 166
Polaroid Palette, 98
Posture, 159–160
Preoccupation, 8, 126, 144, 147, 161
Preparation, 13, 14, 32, 167, 185
Presentations
  beginning, 40–41
  classification by purpose, 5
  cost, 11
  degree of formality, 12
  disadvantages, 10
  ending, 57
  informational type, 5
  middle, 42–56
  motivational type, 6
  objectives, examples of, 7
    uses of, 18
  proposal type, 5
  purposes of, 5, 6, 7, 40
  reference value, 10
  review of, 5
  rooms for, 5
  scope of, 18, 40
  special power, 6
  team, 182–183
  technical vs. business, 5
Probability, 67–68
Projected media, 74–81
Pronunciation, 151–153

Qualifiers, 67–69
Questions, 169–174

Reading
  to an audience, 65, 130, 167
  a speech, 180–182
  vs. listening, 7–12
Real objects as visuals, 83
Rebuttal, 54–55
Recitation behavior, 131
Reductio ad absurdum, 55
Reference, 10, 83
Reflection-type overhead projector, 77
Rehearsal, 178–179
Repetition, 72

Report, 4
Resolution quality of visuals, 98
Retort, 54
Right brain, 103
Room
  acoustics, 119
  arrangement of chairs, 120–122
  lights, 78, 167
  placement of screen, 121–124
  shape and size, 119
  speaker's position, 121–124
  temperature, 118
Rule of eight, 86
Rule of sevens, 100

Sans serif, 92
Scanners, 97
Scheduling the presentation, 18, 32,
  125–126
Schematics, 110–113
Screen
  looking at, 155, 156, 166
  placement, 121–124, 163
Script, 60–90
Sequence, 37, 42, 58
Slip sheets, 122, 165
Smiling, 169
Speech, 3, 179–182
Speechmaker, 175
Stage fright, 136–143
Statistical graphics, 103–111
Strategy, 18
Style, 64–65, 145
Subordination, 36, 42, 58
Surface graph, 109, 110
Suspense, 64
Syllogism, 51–52

Tables, 102–103
Tactics, 31–35
Technical illustrations vs. photographs,
  116
Telephone calls, 4
Temperature of the room, 118

Terminal behavior, 16
Testimonial, 56
Text slides, 100–102
35mm slides, 76, 78–79, 86, 93, 98, 109,
  117, 124, 166–167
Times, best and worst for presentations,
  125–126
Toastmasters, 143
Tone, 168
Transitions, 71, 80, 165
Transmission-type overhead projector,
  77
Typefaces
  Helvetica, 92
  sans serif, 92
  script, 92
  Times Roman, 92
  Univers, 92
Typesetting, 94
Typewritten visuals, 92–93

Unity, 70–71

Vertical bar charts, 103
Video printers, 93
Video projection, 80, 81
Videotape, 79, 185
Visual
  definition, 73
  media, 73–85
Visual triggers, 89, 90
Visualization, 140, 141
Visuals
  characteristics of effective, 84
  as reference source, 10
  for technical presentations, 111, 112,
    116–117, 164
Vocal
  emphasis, 149
  noise, 150–151
  pace, 146–148
  variety, 154–155
Volume, 145–146, 154
VU-graph, 75

Weasel words, 65–68
Whiteboard, 81, 124
Wiring diagrams, 112
Wooden gestures, 158
Word slides, 100–102
Work in communication, 30, 142
Writing, 4, 5, 10
Writing vs. speaking, 5–12

Written reports, 4

You-are-here slide, 72

Zealot, 175
Zones of communication, 145–146
Zoomie case study, 37, 38